THE CONSULTANTS RESOURCEBOOK 2000

KENNEDY INFORMATION

1999 Consultants ResourceBook
Compiled and published by Kennedy Information, LLC,
publishers of: *Consultants News, Global IT Consulting Report, The Directory of Management Consultants, Executive Recruiter News, Human Resource Management News, Recruiting Trends, The Directory of Executive Recruiters, the International Directory of Executive Recruiters,* and *The Directory of Outplacement and Career Management Firms.*

ISBN 1-885922-34-5

Kennedy Information
One Kennedy Place, Route 12 South, Fitzwilliam, NH 03447
Phone: 800-531-0007   603-585-3101
Fax: 603-585-6401
Email: bookstore@kennedyinfo.com
Internet: http:www.kennedyinfo.com
© Copyright 1999 Kennedy Information, LLC

All rights reserved. This publication is a creative work copyrighted by Kennedy Information, LLC and is fully protected by all applicable copyright laws, as well as by misappropriation, trade secret, unfair competition and other applicable laws. The creators, authors and editors of this publication have added value to the underlying factual material herein through one or more of the following: unique and original selection, coordination, expression, arrangement, and classification of the information.

No part of this publication may be reproduced in any form without the express permission of the publisher. Kennedy Information will vigorously defend all of its rights in this publication.

Every effort has been made towards accuracy of the data contained here. Kennedy Information assumes no liability for errors or omissions of any information in this publication.

TABLE OF CONTENTS

ALPHABETICAL LIST OF CATEGORIES vii

INTRODUCTION ix

CONSULTANTS TO CONSULTANTS

    Academic Consultants 3
    Accountants 9
    Training 10
    Venture Capitalists 11

INFORMATION SYSTEMS/COMMUNICATIONS

    Information Systems/Communications 15
    Telecommunications Equipment 16

MARKETING

    Marketing 19
    Advertising Agencies 22
    Corporate Gifts 23
    Events/Meeting Planners 24
    Public Relations Firms 25
    Web Site Promotion 29

OFFICE SUPPORT

    Air Express/Couriers 33
    Answering Services 35
    Business Stationery 36
    Printers 37
    Temporary Staffing 38
    Video Conferencing 40

PRACTICE MANAGEMENT

    Practice Management 45

PRESENTATION TOOLS

    Presentation Graphics 49

PROFESSIONAL DEVELOPMENT

Associations/Networks 53
Executive Education 56
Speakers Bureaus/Agents 60

PROFESSIONAL SERVICES

Professional Services 63
Compensation Advisors 64
Export Advisors 68
Insurance 70
Interpretors & Translators 72
Mergers & Acquisitions Brokers 74
Practice Management Advisors 75

PUBLICATIONS

Publications 81
Books/Directories 82
Magazines/Newsletters 85

RESEARCH

Research 89
Research Databases 90
Research Firms 93
Competitive Intelligence 116

RECRUITING

Business School Career Centers 119
Executive Recruiters 124

SOFTWARE

Software 149
Accounting 152
Business Plan Presentation 155
Contact Management 156
Document Management 157
Intelligence/Expert/Modeling 159
Project Management 162
Time & Billing 164

TRAVEL

Airlines 169
Car Rental Agencies 172

Custom Transportation/Charter Aircraft 173
Frequent Flyer Programs 175
Hotels 189
Temporary Corporate Housing 190

FIRM INDEX 193

INDEX OF ADVERTISERS 204

www.consultingcentral.com

ALPHABETICAL LIST OF CATEGORIES

Academic Consultants	3
Accountants	9
Accounting	152
Advertising Agencies	22
Air Express/Couriers	33
Airlines	169
Answering Services	35
Associations/Networks	53
Books/Directories	82
Business Plan Presentation	155
Business School Career Centers	119
Business Stationery	36
Car Rental Agencies	172
Compensation Advisors	64
Competitive Intelligence	116
CONSULTANTS TO CONSULTANTS	1
Contact Management	156
Corporate Gifts	23
Custom Transportation/Charter Aircraft	173
Document Management	157
Events/Meeting Planners	24
Executive Education	56
Executive Recruiters	124
Export Advisors	68
Frequent Flyer Programs	175
Hotels	189
INFORMATION SYSTEMS/COMMUNICATIONS	13
Insurance	70
Intelligence/Expert/Modeling	158
Interpretors & Translators	72
Magazines/Newsletters	85
MARKETING	17
Mergers & Acquisitions Brokers	74
OFFICE SUPPORT	31
PRACTICE MANAGEMENT	43
Practice Management Advisors	75
Presentation Graphics	49

2000 Consultants ResourceBook / vii

PRESENTATION TOOLS	47
Printers	37
PROFESSIONAL DEVELOPMENT	51
PROFESSIONAL SERVICES	61
Project Management	162
Public Relations Firms	25
PUBLICATIONS	79
RECRUITING	117
RESEARCH	87
Research Databases	90
Research Firms	93
SOFTWARE	147
Speakers Bureaus/Agents	60
Telecommunications Equipment	16
Temporary Corporate Housing	190
Temporary Staffing	38
Time & Billing	164
Training	10
TRAVEL	167
Venture Capitalists	11
Video Conferencing	40
Web Site Promotion	29

INTRODUCTION

Welcome to the second edition of **The Consultants ResourceBook,** the only buyer's guide featuring products and services specifically for management consultants. **The Consultants ResourceBook** was created in response to continual requests from management consultants—many are *Consultants News* subscribers—for information about specialized industry suppliers and vendors.

Consultants use a myriad of software tools, travel sources, information and professional services, marketing approaches, office support and recruiting assistance as they manage their firms and carry out client engagements. The products and services listed in **The Consultants ResourceBook** reflect this broad range. Accordingly, listings run the gamut from niche, industry-specific businesses to vendors who serve broader professional markets that include management consulting.

In compiling **The Consultants ResourceBook,** Kennedy Information endeavored to list products and services that capture the variety of needs management consultants have. We know this listing will grow as consultants inform us about additional services they find useful and suppliers become aware of the ResourceBook as a method to acquaint consultants with their offerings.

Every effort has been made to identify businesses of interest to management consultants, although *Consultants News* does not endorse the use of any product or service listed in the ResourceBook. The contact information we provide is meant to be a starting point for selecting products and services. Some of our listees have taken the opportunity to enhance their listings and elaborate on their capabilities. Please let them know where you found them!

As part of our ongoing effort to produce the best publications possible, we invite your feedback and suggestions on the usefulness, organization and depth of **The Consultants ResourceBook.** We hope the ResourceBook will become an indispensable tool in your successful practice as a management consultant.

Editors

KENNEDY INFORMATION'S
The Directory of Management Consultants

Year 2000, 9th edition, $295.00
800 pages, hardbound

- Profiles 1,823 firms and tells where 7,189 principals work

- Lists 118 services offered and 98 industries served

- Paragraph descriptions of each firm

- Billing and staff-size ranges

- Key principals locator

- Indexed by services, industries, geography, and consultant specialties

- Over 30 pages of valuable information on consulting organizations and advice on working with consulting professionals

---

"...is extremely well-written and complete ...obviously a document that no consulting practice should be without."
　　　　　　　Peter A. Tellegen,
　　　　　Assistant Vice President
　　　Rauscher Pierce Refsnes, Inc.

"...probably the best and the most convenient directory to use..."

　　Business Information Sources
　University of California Press

"In this industry, finding the right peg for the right hole isn't alwasy easy. The directory is a great help."
　　　　　　　　John Costello
　　　　　　in *Nation's Business*

KENNEDY INFORMATION　One Kennedy Place, Route 12 South　Fitzwilliam, NH 03447 USA
800/531-0007　603-585-6544　Fax: 603-585-9555　email: bookstore@kennedyinfo.com

CONSULTANTS TO CONSULTANTS

Academic Consultants

Assessment, Inc.
2600 Van Buren, Suite 2631
Norman, Oklahoma 73072
Phone: (405) 573-9727 (405) 573-9728
Fax: (405) 573-9727
Email: vgettys@ou.edu
Contact: Ms. Vesta S. Gettys
Description: Test development and validation. Expert witness services in hiring, personnel actions. Testing packages for executive selection/promotion.
Products/Services: Psychological Screening/Executive Selection.

Rev. Fr. Brian S. Bainbridge
4 Winifred Street
St. Albans, Victoria 3021
Australia
Phone: 61 3 9366 2146
Fax: 61 3 9366 9876
Email: briansb@mira.net
Contact: Fr. Brian S. Bainbridge
Description: Open space program facilitation, change management.
Products/Services: Open Space Technology.

Benedictine University MBA Program
5700 College Road
Lisle, Illinois 60532-0900
Phone: (630) 829-6217 (630) 829-6219
Fax: (630) 829-6226
Email: bbuchowicz@ben.edu
Contact: Mr. Bruce S. Buchowicz, Ph.D.
Description: We help clients develop and implement strategic change to achieve superior results. A customized approach is used in each engagement; State-of-the-art concepts are employed to yield competitive advantage.
Products/Services: Strategy development and change.

Bentley College
175 Forest Street
Waltham, Massachusetts 02154
Phone: (617) 891-2215 (617) 891-2529
Contact: Mr. Joseph Weiss
Description: 1. Focus groups with top level management to identify and align to strategy and plan. 2. Implementation consulting to execute strategy. 3. Project management seminars.
Products/Services: Strategic alignment; change management; project management.

Bryant College
1150 Dougals Pike
Smithfield, Rhode Island 02917
Phone: (401) 232-6438 (401) 331-0500
Contact: Mr. Kumar Chittipeddi
Description: Strategic planning, Business plans. Top management advisory services.
Products/Services: Management Consulting.

Copenhagen Business School
Dalgas Have 15
Frederiksberg, DK-2000
Denmark
Phone: 45 3815 3009
Fax: 45 3815 3010
Email: mba@mba.dk
Contact: Mr. Hans-Henrik Hansen

Copenhagen Business School
Blaagaardsgade 23B, 2nd floor
Copenhagen, DK-2200
Denmark
Phone: 45 3815 3630
Fax: 45 3815 3635
Email: poulfelt@cbs.dk
WWW: www.cbs.dk
Contact: Mr. Flemming Poulfelt

Cornell University
School of Hotel Administration
Statler Hall
Ithaca, New York 14853
Phone: (607) 255-8361 (607) 273-4738
Fax: (607) 255-4179
Contact: Mr. Craig C. Lundberg
Products/Services: Consulting Skills Workshop.

Sue Canney Davison
P.O. Box 42777
Nairobi,
Kenya
Phone: 254 2 745707
Email: pipal@arcc.or.ke
Contact: Ms. Sue Canney Davison
Description: Management consultants in international teams management development and organizational change.
Products/Services: Pipal International.

Entrepreneurial Strategies
107 South Yellowstone Avenue, Suite C
Bozeman, Montana 59718
Phone: (406) 587-5664
Fax: (406) 586-0396
Contact: Mr. Norris F. Krueger, Jr., Ph.D.
Description: Helping organizations become more entrepreneurial; helping communities become more entrepreneurial; market assessments for 'really new' products/technologies; strategic planning & marketing planning.

Dr. James W. Fairfield-Sonn
12 Essex Industrial Park
P.O. Box 171
Centerbrook, Connecticut 06409-0171
Phone: (860) 767-4979
Fax: (860) 767-7268
Email: fairfield@uhavax.hartford.edu
WWW: www.hartford.edu/fairfield
Contact: Dr. James W. Fairfield-Sonn
Description: Strategic planning, executive development, business analysis and development.

Arnold J. Frigeri
1716 Norma Road
Columbus, Ohio 43229
Phone: (614) 854-0354
Fax: (614) 854-0354
Email: frigeria@franklin.edu
Contact: Arnold J. Frigeri, Ed.D.
Description: Improve performance results through team and organization development change management, strategic formulation and implementation consulting.
Products/Services: Performance Management.

Hispanic North American Center
152 Park Terrace
Sherrill, New York 13461
Phone: (315) 363-1556 (613) 233-3336
Fax: (315) 363-1556
Email: rodriaz@microplus.ca
Contact: Mr. Ren Rodriguez, CEO
Description: To provide international connections and technical support beyond language and cultural barriers to businesses and institutions that want to establish international business operations or institutional links with Spanish, Portuguese and French speaking countries of the Americas and the world.
Products/Services: HNACIBLA.

IBPC, Inc.
P.O. Box 422039
San Francisco, California 94142
Phone: (415) 751-6876
Fax: (415) 668-0250
Email: ibpc@ibpcinc.com
WWW: www.ibpcinc.com
Contact: Mr. Ibrahim Warde, Ph.D.
Description: Publications, Consulting and Training on global banking and finance.

Institute for Intellectual Capital Research
1280 Main Street West, MDG #207
Hamilton, Ontario L8S 4M4
Canada
Phone: (905) 525-9140 ext. 23918
Fax: (905) 521-8995
Email: nbontis@mcmaster.ca
WWW: www.business.mcmaster.ca/mktg/nbontis/ic/
Contact: Dr. Nick Bontis, Ph.D.
Description: Evaluate an organization's knowledge management system by diagnosing organizational learning flows and intellectual capital stocks.
Products/Services: Knowledge Management Audit.

Jamieson Consulting Group
2265 Westwood Boulevard, Suite 310
Los Angeles, California 90064
Phone: (310) 397-8502
Fax: (310) 397-0229
Email: djamieso@pepperdine.edu
Contact: Dr. David W. Jamieson, President
Description: Consulting on change management.
Products/Services: Academic consultant.

Jeanneret & Associates, Inc.
601 Jefferson #3900
Houston, Texas 77002
Phone: (713) 650-6535
Fax: (713) 650-6595
Email: ja02@interserv.com
Contact: Mr. Dick Jeanneret
Description: Human Resource management consulting including selection systems, validation research, psychological assessment, training, performance management, compensation, EEO and expert council on discrimination issues.

Herbert Kierulff
815 West Argand Street
Seattle, Washington 98119
Phone: (206) 285-9106
Fax: (206) 285-8722
Email: hkierulf@spu.edu
WWW: www.spu.edu/depts/sbc
Contact: Mr. Herbert Kierulff
Description: Entrepreneurship, new venture planning and management, turnaround management, financial analysis.
Products/Services: Management Consulting and Education

Korey International Ltd.
55 Tanbark Crescent
Don Mills, Ontario M3B 1N7
Canada
Phone: (416) 445-4968
Fax: (416) 360-3805
Contact: Dr. George Korey, President
Description: International management consulting, strategic planning and management.

A Rao Korukonda
2071 Rio Drive
Allegany, New York 14706
Phone: (716) 373-6860
Fax: (716) 373-2270
Email: akorukon@sbu.edu
Contact: Dr. A. R. Korukonda
Description: Cross-cultural management, management development training and work shops.

McCarty Kilian & Company
16700 County Highway
Chippewa Falls, Wisconsin 54729
Phone: (715) 726-0561
Contact: Mr. Claire McCarty Kilian, Ph.D.
Description: Organizational learning and development, sales, communication, and management training.
Products/Services: The Team Learning Lab, Presentations that work.

Mark A. Mishken
202 Riverside Drive
New York, New York 10025
Phone: (212) 864-4866
Email: mishken@pacevm.dac.edu
Contact: Mr. Mark A. Mishken
Description: Organization development, strategic change, management development.

MIT Sloan School of Management
50 Memorial Drive, E52,557
Cambridge, Massachusetts 02139
Phone: (617) 776-0065 (617) 253-6620
Contact: Mr. Andreas Gast
Description: Specializing in: knowledge management, international transfer of best practice, multi point organizational learning and knowledge transfers in intra-firm networks.
Products/Services: General Consulting: support for consultants, support for management education.

NCA Associates
27 Wampum Road
Narragansett, Rhode Island 02882
Phone: (401) 783-6707 (401) 792-8295
Fax: (401) 874-4312
Email: coates@uriacc.uri.edu
Contact: Dr. Norman Coates
Description: Strategic planning; organizational development and management of change; conference facilitation.

PKT Consulting Forum
Unioninkatu 14
Helsinki, 00130
Finland
Phone: 358 9 7511 7528
Fax: 358 9 7511 7500
WWW: www.kolumbus.fi/pkt
Contact: Mr. Reinhold Enqvist
Description: Service to SMEs, large corporations, organizations, and consultants; where to find help or partners.
Products/Services: Register of 1000 consultants.

Radford University
Department of Psychology
P.O. Box 6946
Radford, Virginia 24142
Phone: (540) 831-5519 (540) 831-5791
Contact: Mr. Mark S. Nagy

Michael P. Sabiers, Ph.D.
15 Primrose Avenue
White Plains, New York 10607-1712
Phone: (914) 683-0120
Email: sabiers@msn.com
Contact: Dr. Michael Sabiers, Ph.D.
Description: Organizational development, change management, team facilitator training.

Thomas Taveggia
2188 Lariat Lane
Walnut Creek, California 94596
Phone: (510) 946-9993
Contact: Mr. Thomas Taveggia
Description: Practice Strategy, Organization and Management, Practice Economics, Compensation.
Products/Services: Academic Consultant.

University of Ballarat
P.O. Box 663
Ballarat, Victoria 3353
Australia
Phone: 61353 279 646
Contact: Ms. Christine O'Connor

University of Chicago
Graduate School Of Business
5605 South Drexel Avenue, #2
Chicago, Illinois 60637
Phone: (773) 256-1441 (312) 879-3579
Email: robert.kenmore@gsb.uchicago.edu
WWW: members.aol.com/rkenmore/index.html
Contact: Mr. Robert Kenmore
Description: Specialized research, analysis, and consulting to organizations in the areas of quality management, org. theory, networks and social structures, international competitiveness, and general operations.
Products/Services: Kenmore Consulting.

University of New Haven
Department Of Psychology
300 Orange Avenue
West Haven, Connecticut 06516
Phone: (203) 932-7289
Contact: Mr. Michael Morris

University of Southern California
Department of Ind. & Sys. Engineering
Los Angeles, California 90089
Phone: (213) 740-4892 (213) 740-6415
Contact: Mr. Gerald Nadler
Description: Principles and process for obtaining significantly better results in strategic planning, system design, improvement programs, conflict management, change management, project management, and facilitation. Based on how leading solution finders think.
Products/Services: Breakthrough Thinking.

University of SW Louisiana
Department of Management/CBA
P.O. Box 43570
Lafayette, Louisiana 70504
Phone: (318) 482-6866 (318) 482-5754
Contact: Mr. Kerry David Carson
Description: Surveying and Health Care Compensation.
Products/Services: Organization Diagnostics.

University of Warwick
MSM Department, Warwick Business School
Coventry, CV4 7AL
United Kingdom
Phone: 44 1203 524541
Contact: Mr. Duncan Angwin
Description: Mergers and acquisitions specialist, strategic management.

Jere E. Yates & Associates

2455 Pacific Coast Hgwy.
Malibu, California 90263
Phone: (310) 456-4237
Fax: (310) 456-4696
Email: jyates@pepperdine.edu
Contact: Jere Yates
Description: Management/organizational development including conflict resolution, team building and stress management.
Products/Services: Organizational/development management

MARKETING

Marketing

Allison, Hull & Malnati, Inc. (AH&M)
P.O. Box 3046
30835 West 10 Mile Road
Farmington Hills, Michigan 48333-3046
Phone: (248) 477-3366
Fax: (248) 477-3070
Email: ahmdet@ahminc.com
WWW: www.ahminc.com
Contact: Ms. Peggy Malnati
Description: We provide marketing & marketing communications services globally to major industrial clients.

American Thermoplastic Company
106 Gamma Drive
Pittsburgh, Pennsylvania 15238-2949
Phone: (800) 245-6600 (412) 967-0900
Fax: (412) 967-9990
Email: atc@binders.com
WWW: www.binders.com
Description: ATC manufactures custom-imprinted ring binders, index sets and related loose-leaf products. Choose from a wide variety of materials, colors and options to meet your specific requirements.
Products/Services: Custom imprinted ring binders.

Business Generation Company
11445 Johns Creek Parkway
Duluth, Georgia 30155
Phone: (770) 813-4911
Email: jockw@GBA.com
WWW: www.gba.com
Contact: Mr. Jock Whitehouse
Description: Design and implementation of customer strategy, combining strategic planning, creativity, & the latest communications technology.

Duncan Direct Associates
16 Elm Street
Peterborough, New Hampshire 03458
Phone: (603) 924-3121
Fax: (603) 924-8511
Email: gduncan@pobox.com
WWW: www.dmworld.com/duncan.html
Contact: Mr. George Duncan
Description: George Duncan is a direct marketing consultant and copywriter who provides response strategies, copy and creative support both to consultants to help them develop their own practices and to their clients as a business partner. From sales letters and brochures to complete lead-generation campaigns—visit our web site and see.

Consultants!

◆ **Do your clients use direct marketing to promote their business?**

◆ **Do *you* use it to promote *yours*?**

George Duncan provides consultants and their clients with insights and guidance, copy and creative support that puts direct response projects on track and on-target, *before* you've spent a ton of money.

Call for expert assistance with
- Sales letters
- Brochures
- Solo dm packages to complete campaigns
  PLUS advice/referrals for
- Lists
- Telemarketing
- Printing & Production and more.

Visit www.dmworld.com/duncan.html for details. Call for our Special Report: "How Much Does it Cost to Do a Mailing?" and "What Kind of Results Should I Expect?" FREE to ResourceBook readers, (a $10 value).

 Duncan Direct Associates
16 Elm Street • Peterborough, NH 03458
Ph: 603-924-3121 • Fx: 603-924-8511
Em: duncandirect@pobox.com

MARKETING

G + A West
17739 NE 13th Street
Bellevue, Washington 98008
Phone: (425) 562-9226
Fax: (425) 562-9120
Contact: Mr. George N. Bukota

Gerald Linda & Associates
2100 Fir Street, Suite 3000
Glenview, Illinois 60025
Phone: (847) 729-3403
Fax: (847) 729-3445
Email: glamktg@aol.com
Contact: Mr. Gerald Linda
Description: Gerald Linda & Associates, a general marketing consultancy, special expertise in marketing communications and research. Offering: marketing strategy, marketing planning, Brand Personality, Brand Boundary Mapping, product development, BrandScrolling Plus, and marketing research services. Gerry Linda is a highly skilled moderator who annually teaches qualitative research in the AMA's School for Research.

National Consultant Registry, LLC
2005 West Centennial Drive
Louisville, Colorado 80027
Phone: (303) 666-0675
Fax: (303) 666-7969
Email: hamilton@h2net.net
Contact: Lyla D. Hamilton, Ph.D.
Description: Expertise in management, marketing, human resources and finance. Specialize in productivity improvement and leadership development. Screened, qualified consultants, professionals and executive coaches.

New Resi Data Marketing, Inc.
172 Broadway
Woodcliff Lake, New Jersey 07675
Phone: (201) 476-1800
Fax: (201) 476-1847
Email: info@newresi.com
WWW: www.newresi.com
Contact: Mr. Glenn Weissman
Description: We specialize in all types of lists.
Products/Services: Mailing Lists.

Paragon Company
5285 Brown Road
P.O. Box 670
Oxford, Ohio 45056
Phone: (513) 523-6700
Fax: (513) 523-6711
Email: info@paragonco.com
Contact: Mr. Ron Lerman
Description: Paragon supports relationship building activities of professional and commercial services firms marketing to chairmen, presidents and direct reports. We help clients build and maintain marketing databases and campaign software to launch high quality, quick-cycle marketing programs. Our creative services, mailshop and call center further support clients marketing to the global corporate community.

Sanchez & Levitan

3191 Coral Way, Suite 510
Miami, Florida 33145
Phone: (305) 442-1586
Email: senlev@shadow.net
Contact: Mr. Fausto Sanchez

Senior Level Communications

234 Littleton Road, Suite 2F
Westford, Massachusetts 01886
Phone: (978) 692-4126
Contact: Mr. Richard A. Gaumer
Description: As door openers, we develop meetings and introductions with the senior management of firms that our clients would find profitable to work with. We can substantially improve the billings of any firm by placing them in front of the decision makers at the right companies.
Products/Services: Business Development for the Consulting Industry.

Advertising Agencies

Bliss Gouverneur & Associates
500 Fifth Avenue, Suite 935
New York, New York 10110-0196
Phone: (212) 840-1661
Fax: (212) 840-1663
Email: jsbliss@aol.com
Contact: Mr. John S. Bliss
Description: Full-service public relations firm specializing in the consulting industry, that has 18 years of experience with professional services. We know how to package and market client ideas.
Products/Services: PR

Consultants in Public Relations SA (TAIPEI)
14F, 256, Hsin Yi Road, Section 4
Taipei,
People's Republic of China
Phone: 886 2 700 6876
Contact: Mrs. Irene E. Holmes
Description: Consultants in corporate communications, marketing and training. (Also, Holmes and Associates Limited)

Smart Solutions Marketing Inc.
7154 North University Drive, Suite 276
Ft. Lauderdale, Florida 33309
Phone: (954) 726-7070
Fax: (954) 724-3390
Email: smartsol@paradise.net
Contact: Ms. Lori Chester
Description: Consulting and developing growth and marketing strategies for all size businesses.
Products/Services: Growth & Marketing Strategies

Wolfbayne Communications
P.O. Box 50287
Colorado Springs, Colorado 80949-0287
Phone: (719) 593-8032
Email: kimmik@wolfbayne.com
WWW: www.wolfbayne.com
Contact: Ms. Kim M. Bayne
Description: High tech marketing communication consulting and implementation public relations, and internet marketing.
Products/Services: High Tech Marketing Communications.

Corporate Gifts

Navarro, Kim & Associates
529 North Charles Street, Suite 202
Baltimore, Maryland 21201-5047
Phone: (410) 837-6317
Fax: (410) 837-6317
Contact: Mr. Beltran Navarro
Description: We act as an interface between individuals and firms and non-traditional ethnic communities, (Latinos, Asians, etc). Our social project expertise includes campaigns, community outreach and design of messages that are language and culturally sensitive.
Products/Services: Social Project Design and Management.

Vermont Specialty Products, Inc.
216 Battery Street
Burlington, Vermont 05401
Phone: (802) 864-7010
Fax: (802) 660-9564
Contact: Mr. Dee Deluca, President
Description: We reproduce your image, museum quality, on 400,000 different products.
Products/Services: Corporate Gifts.

Events/Meeting Planners

International Events, Inc.
P. O. Box 272817
Tampa, Florida 33688-2817
Phone: (727) 372-2868 (877) 3-EVENTS
Fax: (727) 372-2867
Email: events@gte.net
WWW: www.iei-corp.com
Contact: Ms. Mary Ellen Upton
Description: The best solution to your outsourcing needs . . . International Events, Inc.

Http://www.vizatours.com

"Where Leaders Meet Leaders"

Promoting World Trade and Economic Development through Corporate Tours

International Events, Inc.
P.O. Box 272817
Tampa Fl 33688-2817
Toll Free: 1-877-3-EVENTS
Phone: 1-727-372-2868
Fax: 1-727-372-2867
E-Mail: events@gte.net

Public Relations Firms

AH&M Marketing Communications
150 North Street, Suite 35
Pittsfield, Massachusetts 01201
Phone: (413) 448-2260
Fax: (413) 445-4026
Email: ahm@ahminc.com
Contact: Mr. Dallas Hull, Principal
Description: Industrial business-to-business marketing communications: Boston, Detroit, Cleveland offices.

Associates Newsletter Bureau
1330 Berkshire Lane
Grayslake, Illinois 60015
Phone: (847) 543-1090
Fax: (847) 543-1089
Email: jleman@interaccess.com
Contact: Mr. Jim Leman
Description: Corporate newsletter, P.R. and sales promotion services.

Barnette & Associates/PR Alabama
2800 Zelda Road, Suite 2007
Montgomery, Alabama 36106
Phone: (334) 277-3133
Fax: (334) 277-1339
Email: cbarnette@aol.com
Contact: Mr. Charles Barnette, APR
Description: Projects welcome! Member PRSA Counselors Academy.

Bliss Gouverneur & Associates
500 Fifth Avenue, Suite 935
New York, New York 10110-0196
Phone: (212) 840-1661
Fax: (212) 840-1663
Email: jsbliss@aol.com
Contact: Mr. John S. Bliss
Description: Full-service public relations firm specializing in the consulting industry, that has 18 years of experience with professional services. We know how to package and market client ideas.
Products/Services: PR

Bradley Marketing Group
555 Skokie Boulevard, Suite 400
Northbrook, Illinois 60062
Phone: (847) 412-9400
Fax: (847) 412-9401
Email: bmg@bradleymarketing.com
WWW: www.bradleymarketing.com
Contact: Ms. Kim A. Bradley, President
Description: A full service marketing comunications firm.
Products/Services: Public Relations Firm

Byrne Johnson Inc.
3010 LBJ Freeway, Suite 1300
Dallas, Texas 75234
Phone: (972) 481-1946
Fax: (972) 481-1932
Email: byrnejohnson@bji.com
WWW: www.bji.com
Contact: Mr. Richard J. Johnson
Description: Strategic marketing counsel and creative services.
Products/Services: Marketing Communications Services.

MARKETING • PUBLIC RELATIONS FIRMS

Kelley Chunn & Associates
17 Grovenor Road, Suite 2L
Boston, Massachusetts 02130
Phone: (617) 524-8529
Fax: (617) 524-1365
Email: KChunn935@aol.com
Contact: Ms. Kelley Chunn
Description: Kelley Chunn is principal of Kelley Chunn & Associates, a state-certified regional, national and international consultancy based in Boston, MA. Their mission is to help businesses, nonprofits and individuals develop multicultural, cause-related marketing and public relations strategies that work. They can be reached at 617-524-8529.

Consultants in Public Relations SA (TAIPEI)
14F, 256, Hsin Yi Road, Section 4
Taipei,
People's Republic of China
Phone: 886 2 700 6876
Contact: Mrs. Irene E. Holmes
Description: Consultants in corporate communications, marketing and training. (Also, Holmes and Associates Limited)

Eisen & Associates
1110 Longshore Avenue
Philadelphia, Pennsylvania 19111
Phone: (215) 745-4168
Fax: (215) 745-5348
Email: greatpr@philly.infi.net
Contact: Mr. Edward N. Eisen
Description: We create the #1 rainmaking tool: free publicity.
Products/Services: Publicity, Special Events, Strategic Marketing, Advertising.

Fuessler Group Inc.
288 Shawmut Avenue
Boston, Massachusetts 02118
Phone: (617) 451-9383
Fax: (617) 451-5950
Email: fuessler@fuessler.com
WWW: www.fuessler.com
Contact: Mr. Rolf Fuessler
Description: PR and marketing communications for professional service firms.
Products/Services: Marketing/communications consulting.

Information Counselors, Inc.
8 Sunset Hill, Box 88
Bethel, Connecticut 06801
Phone: (203) 797-0307
Fax: (203) 798-7763
Contact: Mr. Warren Owens
Description: Publicity for growth companies.
Products/Services: PR.

Anne Klein & Associates, Inc.
Three Greentree Centre, Suite 200
Marlton, New Jersey 08053
Phone: (609) 988-6560
Fax: (609) 988-6564
Email: mailroom@akleinpr.com
WWW: www.akleinpr.com
Contact: Gerhart L. Klein, Esq.
Description: A national public relations firm based in the Philadelphia region.

Ronald Levitt Associates
141 Sevilla Avenue
Miami, Florida 33134
Phone: (305) 443-3223 (954) 349-2596
Email: rla@net.com
Contact: Mr. Howard Levitt
Description: General publicity/governmental relations/advertising consulting.
Products/Services: Public Relations Consultants.

PUBLIC RELATIONS FIRMS • MARKETING

Littman & Associates
4621 Bentley Place
Duluth, Georgia 30096
Phone: (770) 447-5471
Fax: (770) 263-8123
Email: mlittman@aol.com
Contact: Ms. Mindy Littman, President
Description: Marketing and public relations services for high-tech businesses.
Products/Services: Public Relations Firms

The Londre Company, Inc.
3365 Barham Boulevard
Los Angeles, California 90068
Phone: (213) 851-8230
Fax: (213) 851-4427
Email: londrepat@aol.com
WWW: www.londre.com
Contact: Ms. Patti Londre, President
Description: Specialists in marketing PR for food, beverage and consumer products.
Products/Services: Public Relations.

The Lukaszewski Group Inc.
Ten Bank Street, Suite 530
White Plains, New York 10606-1933
Phone: (914) 681-0000
Fax: (914) 681-0047
Email: tlg@e911.com
WWW: www.e911.com
Contact: Mr. James E. Lukaszewski
Description: Management consultants in crisis communications.

The Pollack PR Marketing Group
1901 Avenue of the Stars, Suite 1040
Los Angeles, California 90067
Phone: (310) 556-4443
Fax: (310) 286-2350
Email: info@ppmgcorp.com
Contact: Ms. Noemi Pollack

Philip G. Ryan Inc.
80 Eighth Avenue
New York, New York 10011
Phone: (212) 206-0033
Fax: (212) 206-1325
Email: PGRyan@aol.com
Contact: Mr. Phil Ryan
Description: Founded in 1981, Philip G. Ryan, Inc. is one of New York's leading public relations firms specializing in the corporate and professional services sector.
Products/Services: PR.

Selz/Seabolt Communications Inc.
1620 Eye Street NW, Suite 220
Washington, District of Columbia 20006-4005
Phone: (202) 775-8070
Fax: (202) 223-8323
Email: sscdc@aol.com
Contact: Mr. George M. Kroloff, Senior Vice President-Eastern Region
Description: Constituency building, meeting management, marketing.
Products/Services: US & International/PR Public Affairs.

D. J. Storch & Associates, Inc.
3060 North Beach Road
Englewood, Florida 34223
Phone: (941) 474-5909
Fax: (941) 474-5640
Email: dj3060@aol.com
Contact: Mr. Donald J. Storch, President
Description: Healthcare/pharmaceutical public relations/issue and crisis management.
Products/Services: Public Relations.

L. C. Williams & Associates, Inc.
150 North Michigan Avenue, Suite 3800
Chicago, Illinois 60601
Phone: (312) 565-3900
Fax: (312) 565-1770
Email: lou@lcwa.com
Contact: Mr. Louis C. Williams
Description: A full service public relations & research counseling firm.
Products/Services: Public relations, research.

Zigman-Joseph-Stephenson
100 East Wisconsin Avenue
Milwaukee, Wisconsin 53202
Phone: (414) 273-4680
Fax: (414) 273-3158
Email: johnr@zjs.com
WWW: pr@zjs.com
Contact: Mr. John Rumpf
Description: Public relations, issues and corporate reputation management counsel since 1958.
Products/Services: Public Relations Agency.

Web Site Promotion

Adwoa Boateng
620 Park Avenue, Box 221
Rochester, New York 14607
Phone: (716) 473-1242 (703) 416-6580
Email: nanaachia@aol.com
Contact: Mr. Adwoa A. Boateng
Description: Electronic Information Access and Management Specialist. Expertise/Specialties: 1. Technical, Medical, Business information. 2. Endures needs assessment 3. Database design and content knowledge. 4. Web Home page design and content knowledge.

CRL Network Services Headquarters
One Kearny Street
San Francisco, California 94108
Phone: (415) 837-5300
Fax: (415) 392-9000
Email: sales@crl.com
WWW: www.crl.com/
Contact: Ms. Laura Seymour
Description: CRL Network focuses on dedicated, high-bandwidth internet and intranet connectivity solutions to businesses, universities and ISPs. CRL is one of only a handful of data networking companies that provides both private, managed frame relay services, and first-tier internet access over the same network, through the same physical connection. TCP/IP and packet switching are the fundamentals of the companies network technology. As the next generations of communications networks are built, CRL is well positioned to offer solutions for the design, construction and management of highly complex data networking projects.
Products/Services: Business Networking Solutions.

Deyo Group/Online
27 Empire Drive, Suite 200
St. Paul, Minnesota 55103
Phone: (612) 602-3139
Fax: (612) 602-3130
Email: deyogroup@aol.com
Contact: Mr. Steve Deyo, President
Description: The Deyo Group/Online bears a roster of nationally known independent consultants who specialize in evaluating or directing the development or implementation of client/server, workgroup, Internet, intranet, networking, agent/scripting, and mobile technologies as well as product launches and the formulation of business or marketing strategy, especially relating to online, Internet, World Wide Web, electronic publishing, or digital commerce ventures.

Management Consultant Network International
858 Longview Road
Burlingame, California 94010-6974
Phone: (650) 342-5259
Fax: (650) 344-5005
Email: mcni@mcni.com
WWW: www.mcni.com
Contact: Mr. E. Michael Shays
Description: MCNI is a constellation of web sites and directories listing information world-wide about management consultants, including consultants by expertise, associations, publications and other resources for the consultant, client or reporter.
Products/Services: An individual page for a management consultant listing 600 words that can be searched for a match to a client need.

Matterform Media
500 North Guadalupe St., Suite G333
Santa Fe, New Mexico 87501
Phone: (505) 747-1220
Fax: (505) 747-1769
Email: design@matterform.com
WWW: www.matterform.com
Contact: Mr. Michael Herrick, Lead Designer
Description: New designs and re-designs. Sites for management consultants our specialty.
Products/Services: Web Site Design.

PSINet
510 Huntmar Park Drive
Herndon, Virginia 20170-5100
Phone: (800) 395-1056 (703) 904-4100
Email: info@psi.com
WWW: www.psi.net
Contact: Mr. Tony Kelly
Products/Services: InterFrame, InterMAN®, LAN on Demand, InterRamp, PSIWeb.

Sakson & Taylor, Inc.
4300 Aurora Avenue North, Suite 100
Seattle, Washington 98103
Phone: (206) 632-6931
Fax: (206) 632-6927
Email: carolp@sakson.com
WWW: www.sakson.com/index.htm
Contact: Ms. Carol Peterson
Description: Sakson & Taylor develops multimedia information systems, websites, online help systems, training, materials and software documentation. We also provide technical communications contract employees.
Products/Services: Online Information and Web Design.

Topeka
2295 Francisco Street, Suite 102
San Francisco, California 94123
Phone: (415) 474-1297
Fax: (415) 474-1296
Email: topeka@well.com
WWW: www.well.com/user/topeka
Contact: Mr. Bill Rapp
Description: Topeka is a multi-faceted marketing solutions firm, whose specialty is the re-invigoration of stale, boring, lifeless presentations. From attention-grabbing video to interactive multimedia to dynamic website design, Topeka has the creative firepower and marketing savvy to make people sit up and take notice.
Products/Services: Marketing Design.

Universes Network
2735 North Clark Street, Suite 143
Chicago, Illinois 60614
Phone: (312) 503-8441
Email: link@universes.com
WWW: www.universes.com
Contact: Mr. Anthony Diaz
Description: Universes Network is a reliable company with skills on HTML, CGI scripting, Active-X, databases, web site design and project management, graphic design and layout, interactive marketing campaigns and Web Translations to and from English to French, Spanish and German.
Products/Services: Web Site Designers.

OFFICE SUPPORT

Air Express/Couriers

AB Express
8519 East 21st Street
Kansas City, Missouri 64126-3085
Phone: (800) 848-9827 (816) 461-4040
WWW: www.abexpress.com/

Advanced Express
115 Clermont Avenue
P.O. Box 23292
Alexandria, Virginia 22304-9329
Phone: (703) 751-6100
Fax: (703) 751-6121
Contact: Mr. Joseph Fishman
Description: Worldwide freight expeditery specializing in association freight services. Call for rate quote.

Airborne Express
P.O. Box 662
Seattle, Washington 98111
Phone: (800) 247-2676
Email: cac.web@airborne.com
WWW: www.airborne-express.com/
Contact: Mr. Tom Branigan
Description: Airborne Express is the third largest and fastest growing air express delivery carrier in America,
Products/Services: Air Express Delivery.

Burlington Air Express
16808 Armstrong Avenue
Irvine, California 92714
Phone: (800) 528-8110

DHL Worldwide Express
333 Twin Dolphin Drive
Redwood City, California 94065
Phone: (800) 225-5345 (415) 593-7474
WWW: www.dhl.com
Description: International air express delivery of documents and packages of any weight or size.

Federal Express
2003 Corporate Avenue MS1862
Memphis, Tennessee 38132
Phone: (800) 463-3339 (901) 395-3610
Fax: (901) 395-3610
WWW: www.fedex.com

Greyhound Package Express
P.O. Box 660606
Dallas, Texas 75266-0606
Phone: (800) 739-5020 (972) 789-7440
Email: package@greyhound.com
WWW: www.greyhound.com/package.html

Mail Boxes Etc.
300 Carlsbad Village Drive
Carlsbad, California 92008
Phone: (619) 434-9933

Purolator Courier
5995 Avebury Road
Mississauga, Ontario L5P 1C2
Canada
Phone: (888) 744-7123
WWW: www.purolator.ca/index.html

OFFICE SUPPORT • AIR EXPRESS/COURIERS

United Parcel Service
55 Glenn Lake Parkway
14841 Sweitzer Lane
Atlanta, Georgia 30328
Phone: (800) 742-5877 (301) 604-7232
WWW: www.ups.com

Answering Services

The Office Alternative
1455 South Reynolds Road
Toledo, Ohio 43615-7400
Phone: (419) 389-1212 (419) 389-1216
Fax: (419) 389-9460
Contact: Ms. Kelly Stiner
Description: Live telephone answering, VM, mail receiving, paging, secretarial support, accounting services.
Products/Services: The Office Alternative.

Office Centre
250 South Stemmons, Third Floor
Lewisville, Texas 75067
Phone: (972) 436-9523
Contact: Mr. Sam Rosson, President
Description: Offices, secretarial services, answering services (executive suites).
Products/Services: Executive suites offices with services provided.

Business Stationery

Fidelity Graphics, Inc.
285 Windermere Ave.
Lansdowne, Pennsylvania 19050-1153
Phone: (610) 622-6223
Fax: (610) 622-6122
Email: www.pjdriscolli.juno
Contact: Ms. Clare J. Driscoll
Description: All printing needs from conception to completion with design and delivery.
Products/Services: Office Printing- Custom/Stock

1-800-Batteries
2301 Robb Drive
Reno, Nevada 89523
Phone: (800) 228-8374 (702) 746-6140
Email: hawk@1800Batteries.com
WWW: www.1800Batteries.com
Contact: Mr. Ken Hawk
Description: Batteries & tools for mobile professionals. Over 6,000 models of laptop PC, cellular phone, camcorder and cordless phone batteries, adapters and chargers.
Products/Services: Rechargeable batteries, adapters, car cords for portable PC.

Black Box Catalog
1000 Park Drive
Lawrence, Pennsylvania 15055
Phone: (800) 552-6816 (412) 746-5500
Email: info@blackbox.com
WWW: www.blackbox.com

Egghead
22705 East Mission
Liberty Lake, Washington 99019-8553
Phone: (800) EGG-HEAD
WWW: www.egghead.com

Global Computer Supplies
11 Harbor Park Drive, Department RF
Port Washington, New York 11050
Phone: (800) 845-6225 (516) 625-6200
Fax: (516) 625-6683
WWW: www.globalcomputer.com

INMAC
55 United States Avenue
P.O. Box 69
Gibbsboro, New Jersey 08026
Phone: (800) 547-5444
Fax: (800) 972-3210

Macwarehouse (PC Warehouse)
1720 Oak Street
P.O. Box 3013
Lakewood, New Jersey 08701-5926
Phone: (800) 981-9196 (800) 255-6227
WWW: www.warehouse.com

PC Connection, Inc.
528 Route 13 South
Milford, New Hampshire 03055-3442
Phone: (603) 423-2278
Fax: (603) 446-7791
WWW: www.pcconnection.com

PC Zone (Mac Zone)
707 South Grady Way
Renton, Washington 98055-3233
Phone: (800) 258-2088 (800) 248-0800
WWW: www.zones.com

Printers

Morris Graphics Inc.
660 North Broad Street
Woodbury, New Jersey 08096-1708
Phone: (609) 845-4980
Fax: (609) 853-5787
Email: jeff@morrisgraphics.com
WWW: www.morrisgraphics.com
Contact: Mr. Jeff Morris
Description: Single color through multi-color printing. Brochures, newsletters, product literature. Marketing and advertising materials. Imprinted promotional products.
Products/Services: Printing and promotional products.

Temporary Staffing

ACSYS Resources Inc.
1300 Market Street, Suite 501
Wilmington, Delaware 19801
Phone: (302) 658-6181
Fax: (302) 658-6244
Email: dom@acsysresources.com
WWW: www.acsysresources.com
Contact: Mr. Domenic L. Vacca
Description: Permanent and temporary contract staffing for accounting, finance, financial services, and data processing.
Products/Services: Professional perm/temp staffing.

The Ascher Group
7 Becker Farm Road
Roseland, New Jersey 07068
Phone: (973) 597-1900
Fax: (973) 597-1911
Contact: Ms. Susan Ascher
Description: The Ascher Group, founded in 1981, is a generalist firm which recruits middle and senior level managers for a variety of disciplines and industries. We also offer temporary and strategic staffing services.
Products/Services: Executive staffing and traditional hires.

DFG Staffing Consultants, Inc.
25 East Spring Valley Avenue
Maywood, New Jersey 07607
Phone: (201) 845-7700
Fax: (201) 845-5164
Email: postmaster@data-finders.com
WWW: www.data-finders.com
Contact: Mr. Thomas J. Credidio
Description: Executive Recruiters of Information Technology Consultants for both "permanent" and "temporary" contract consulting opportunities.

The Executive Source Inc.
55 Fifth Avenue, 19th Floor
New York, New York 10003-4301
Phone: (212) 691-5505
Fax: (212) 691-9839
Email: TES5505@aol.com
Contact: Ms. Sarah J. Marks
Description: We focus on providing interim and permanent senior human resources professionals specializing in financial services and insurance.

FM Staffing, Inc.
18 East 53rd Street, 6th Floor
New York, New York 10022
Phone: (212) 486-0010
Fax: (212) 371-2030
Email: fmstffng@aol.com
Contact: Ms. Judith M. Peterson
Description: We place permanent and temporary graphics operators, technical support personnel, workflow managers and proofreaders. We design presentation formats and templates, offer application selection assistance, installation and training, and select and install graphics workstations, servers, printers and other network hardware.
Products/Services: Temporary staffing.

KPA Associates, Inc.
150 Broadway, Suite 1900
New York, New York 10038
Phone: (212) 964-3640
Fax: (212) 964-6959
Email: lenadams@pipline.com
Contact: Mr. Len Adams

Robert T. Morton Associates, Inc.
35 Fields Pond Road
Weston, Massachusetts 02493
Phone: (781) 899-4904
Fax: (781) 899-6514
Email: rtmorton@aol.com
Contact: Mr. Robert T. Morton
Description: Retained search plus contract recruiting provider for high technology—engineering (all), sales, marketing, manufacturing, finance, etc.

Professional Support Inc.
501 John James Audubon Parkway
One Towne Centre, Suite 402
West Amherst, New York 14228
Phone: (716) 688-0235
Fax: (716) 688-0239
Email: buffalo@psi4jobs.com
WWW: www.psi4jobs.com
Contact: Mr. Greg Eastmer
Description: Executive recruiting (retainer search), in accounting & data processing, disciplines; contract and rent-to-own programs, temporary clerical & DP operational services; contract data processing (project) services, individual & group outplacement services, training programs, facilities planning & disaster recovery services.

Southwestern Professional Services
2451 Atrium Way
Nashville, Tennessee 37214
Phone: (615) 391-2586
Fax: (615) 231-4000
Email: truitt@southwestern.com
WWW: www.careerenhancer.com
Contact: Mr. Tom Truitt
Description: We specialize in the placement of management consulting professionals within Big 5 and large specialty boutiques. Our emphasis includes enterprise resource planning (ERP) packages including SAP, Oracle and PeopleSoft. Additionally we place similar personnel within Fortune 500 Companies throughout the United States.

Video Conferencing

American Teleconferencing Services, Ltd.
10955 Lowell Avenue, Suite 500
Overland Park, Kansas 66210
Phone: (800) 234-2546 (913) 661-0700
Fax: (913) 661-9897
Email: therbic@atsgroup.com
WWW: www.atsgroup.com
Contact: Ms. Teresa Herbic
Description: ATS is a leading provider of conference calls and group communications services worldwide.

Business Development Group, Inc.
107 Miller
Ann Arbor, Michigan 48104
Phone: (734) 741-4150 (248) 552-0821
Fax: (248) 552-1924
Email: njsimon@aol.com
Contact: Mr. Neil Simon
Description: Our mission is to assist organizations to design their own evolution through a highly participative process that integrates people, technology, and work systems. Our firm works with organizations to innovate, design or redesign departments, divisions or the entire organization in order to optimize organizational performance.
Products/Services: Organizational design and development.

Facilitate.com
426 North Hope Avenue
Santa Barbara, California 93110
Phone: (805) 682-6939
Fax: (805) 682-6279
WWW: www.facilitate.com
Contact: Mr. Michael McCall
Description: Facilitate.com is a powerful and easy to use tool designed to enable work groups and organizations to collaborate the meeting and conference process.
Products/Services: Facilitate.com.

Networkmci Conferencing
8750 West Bryn Mawr Avenue, Suite 501
Chicago, Illinois 60631
Phone: (800) 475-5000 (773) 399-1700
WWW: www.mci.com
Contact: Ms. Vicki Moliana
Products/Services: NetworkMCI Videoconferencing.

Picturetel Corporation
100 Minuteman Road
Andover, Massachusetts 01810
Phone: (978) 292-5000
Fax: (978) 292-3000
WWW: www.pictel.com
Contact: Mr. Nettie Casey
Products/Services: Live200.

Polycom, Inc.
2584 Junction Avenue
San Jose, California 95134-1902
Phone: (408) 526-9000 (800) 765-9266
Fax: (408) 474-2542
Email: sales@polycom.com
WWW: www.polycom.com
Contact: Ms. Gloria Consola
Description: Polycom is a leading provider of high quality easy-to-use teleconferencing products.
Products/Services: SoundStation.

Vista Satellite Communications, Inc.
305 South Andrews Avenue, Suite 900
Ft. Lauderdale, Florida 33301
Phone: (954) 525-7884
Fax: (954) 525 7868
Email: info@vistasat.com
WWW: www.vistasat.com
Contact: Mr. Jay Lebowitz
Description: VISTA is a full-service satellite networking, transmission, videoconferencing and meeting planning company that services all levels of the broadcast, cable, corporate, education and healthcare industries.
Products/Services: Videoconferencing, Satellite Networking, meeting planning, full-time & occasional use satellite capacity (international & domestic).

PRACTICE MANAGEMENT

Practice Management

M. A. Raphael & Associates
429 Kennedy Road
Windsor, Connecticut 06095
Phone: (860) 688-2800
Email: mraphae80ix.netcom.com
Contact: Dr. Michael Raphael
Description: Psychological assessment; organization consulting; seminars.

PRESENTATION TOOLS

Presentation Graphics

PEP Enterprises
7325 North 16th Street, Suite 100
Phoenix, Arizona 85020
Phone: (602) 944-2080
Email: pep@getnet.com
WWW: www.getnet.com/pep
Contact: Ms. Janice Borovay
Description: PEP provides consulting services for corporations, information technology user groups, professional associations and not-for-profit organizations in the areas of corporate meeting planning, performance enhancement programs, membership development and retention, marketing, volunteer leadership development and board governance.

PROFESSIONAL DEVELOPMENT

Associations/Networks

American Consultants League
30466 Prince William Street
Princess Anne, Maryland 21853
Phone: (410) 651-4869
Fax: (410) 651-4885
Contact: Mr. Hubert Bermont, Executive Director
Description: Training professionals in the business of consulting.
Products/Services: Consultants Association

Association of Management Consulting Firms
380 Lexingtin Avenue, Suite 1700
New York, New York 10168
Phone: (212) 551-7887
Fax: (212) 551-7934
Email: info@amcf.org **WWW:** www.amcf.org
Contact: Ms. Elizabeth Kovacs, President
Description: The Association of Management Consulting Firms is the premiere professional association for management consulting firms, representing the profession through our member firms worldwide. Each of our members pledges to adhere to the AMCF Code of Ethics and to meet the highest standards of Professional Practice, based on the recommendations of clients and peers.
Products/Services: AMCF

ASSOCIATION OF
MANAGEMENT
CONSULTING
FIRMS

380 LEXINGTON AVENUE,
SUITE 1700
NEW YORK, NY 10168
TEL: 212 551-7887
FAX: 212 551-7934
WWW.AMCF.ORG

70 years . . . helping our member firms be highly succeessful in their profession.

AMCF serves the senior management teams of
firms that demonstrate their ability to serve
clients with the highest standards
of objectivity, integrity and competence.

Member services: networking, training, industry
research, legislative monitoring,
referral service, and customized programs
to help member firms succeed.

1999 Annual Fall Meeting: September 22 - 24
Playing To Win: How The Fittest Firms
Compete and Survive
Westin Saint Francis Hotel, San Francisco, CA

PROFESSIONAL DEVELOPMENT

Institute of Management Consultants

is committed to leading the management consulting profession by serving, representing and certifying management consultants.

offers professional development through over 200 national and regional events, workshops and seminars throughout the United States.

awards the Certified Management Consultant (CMC) designation, the preeminent certification in the profession.

Visit the IMC website at http://www.imcusa.org for the CMC referral list and other useful information.

IMC 521 FIFTH AVENUE
NEW YORK, NY 10175-3598
Phone 212-697-8262   Fax 212-949-6571

Institute of Management Consultants
521 Fifth Avenue, 35th Floor
New York, New York 10175-3598
Phone: (212) 697-8262 (800) 221-2557
Fax: (212) 949-6571
Email: office@imcusa.org
WWW: www.imcusa.org
Contact: Ms. Aline Cajuste

International Council of Management Consulting Institutes
858 Longview Road, Suite 200
Burlingame, California 94010-6974
Phone: (800) 568-5668 (650) 342-2250
Fax: (650) 344-5005
Email: icmci@icmci.org
WWW: icmci.org/icmci/
Contact: Mr. E. Michael Shays
Description: The international association of national institutes that certifies individual management consultants with the designation CMC.
Products/Services: World-wide standards for management consulting practice.

National Bureau of Certified Consultants (NBCC)
2728 Fifth Avenue
San Diego, California 92103
Phone: (619) 297-2207
Fax: (619) 296-3580
Email: nationalbureau@worldnet.att.net
WWW: expert-market.com/nbpmc
Contact: Mr. James R. Bickmann, Director of Professional Services
Description: We are an association of certified consultants to management with members in 46 states and 10 countries. Request info kit #10 at no cost or obligation.
Products/Services: Association

National Speakers Association
1500 South Priest Drive
Tempe, Arizona 85281
Phone: (602) 968-2552
Email: nsamain@aol.com
WWW: www.nsaspeaker.org
Description: NSA is an international association of more than 3,700 members dedicated to advancing the art and value of experts who speak professionally.

PEP Enterprises

7325 North 16th Street, Suite 100
Phoenix, Arizona 85020
Phone: (602) 944-2080
Email: pep@getnet.com
WWW: www.getnet.com/pep
Contact: Ms. Janice Borovay
Description: PEP provides consulting services for corporations, information technology user groups, professional associations and not-for-profit organizations in the areas of corporate meeting planning, performance enhancement programs, membership development and retention, marketing, volunteer leadership development and board governance.

Executive Education

American Media, Inc.
4900 University Avenue
West Des Moines, Iowa 50266
Phone: (800) 262-2557 (515) 224-0919
Fax: (515) 224-0256
Email: ami@ammedia.com
WWW: www.ammedia.com
Contact: Mr. Steve DeWall
Description: American Media offers more than 250 training videos, audios, self-study books, and multimedia products including the Just-In-Time Information Performance Support System, on a wide-range of employee performance topics including: sexual harassment, interviewing, customer service, diversity, legal issues, and much more. AMI also offers custom-designed training services including On-Site Training & Consulting, Video Rental Program, Self-Directed Book Program, Volume Purchase Program and Custom Video and Multimedia Production Services.
Products/Services: Training Videos.

Bar Ilan University
School of Business Administration
Ramat-Gan, 52900
Israel
Phone: 972 3 531 8903
Fax: 972 3 535 3182
Email: caspia@mail.biu.ac.il
Contact: Mr. Amnon Caspi

Business Advantage, Inc.
4900 University Avenue
West Des Moines, Iowa 50266-6769
Phone: (800) 305-9004
Fax: (800) 305-8997
Contact: Ms. Alison Collette
Description: Business Advantage, Incorporated, a division of American Media, Inc., offers over 200 self-study training videos, audios, and books. Most products $99 or less. Training topics include all core HR issues, communication skills, professional development, management skills, computer training, sales training, legal issues and more.
Products/Services: Training Videos, Audios, Books.

Community-L, Inc.
Route 2, Box 4723-C
Berryville, Virginia 22611
Phone: (540) 955-1894
Fax: (540) 955-1822
Contact: Dr. Clyde Croswell
Description: Professional services that develop organizational learning and leadership for individuals and teams in business, government, and non-profit organizations to improve effectiveness and efficiency: services focus on knowledge, self-organizing systems, and appreciative ecology.
Products/Services: Human Resource and Organization Development.

William D. Criddle, Ph.D.
411 University Street, #1200
Seattle, Washington 98101
Phone: (206) 624-1552 (206) 842-4091
Fax: (206) 467-0212
Email: LCRIDL@U.Washington.EDU
Contact: Mr. William D. Criddle
Description: Family business consulting; executive coaching, management skill building; crisis consulting, management retreats, management skill building.
Products/Services: Managerial Psychologist.

The Finnie Group
3636 South Geyer, Suite 240
St. Louis, Missouri 63127
Phone: (314) 821-5099
Fax: (314) 821-4547
Email: 102651.3176@compuserve.com
Contact: Mr. William C. Finnie
Description: The two day strategy development program helps the top management team develop a vision, a strategy for achieving the vision and an implementation plan to reach 100% of potential.
Products/Services: Strategic and long range planning.

Hart & Associates, Inc.
4201 Marvin Place, Suite 100
Raleigh, North Carolina 27609-5951
Phone: (919) 782-8739
Fax: (919) 571-0231
Email: JGHartCMC@aol.com
WWW: jghart.mcni.com
Contact: Mr. J. G. (Jerry) Hart, CMC
Description: Our focus is on Management and GainSharing. We help organizations achieve superior performance by using proven, practical, easy-to-apply, management improvement techniques which produce tangible results on the bottom line. Our new Fundamentals Revisited package includes Logic-Flow Planning, Outcome Expectations Exercise, ShirtSleeves MBO and GainSharing. These provide the basic organizational foundations for building sound, practical plans plus the positive motivational climate which encourages and rewards total-teamwork and exceptional performance.
Products/Services: Fundamentals Re-visited., GainSharing Design & Implementation., Executive Counseling.

Human Resource Development Press
22 Amherst Road
Amherst, Massachusetts 01002
Phone: (800) 822-2801
Fax: (413) 253-3490
Email: hrdpress@hrdpress.com
WWW: www.hrdpress.com
Contact: Mr. Randy Phillips
Description: HRD Press publishes off-the-shelf assessments, workshops, and books for high performance training. Topics include leadership, team building, customer service, sales and more.
Products/Services: Off-the-shelf assessments and workshops.

IMD-International Institute for Management Development

Ch. de Bellerive 23
P.O. Box 915
Lausanne, CH-1001
Switzerland
Phone: 41 21 618 0342
Fax: 41 21 618 0715
Email: info@imd.ch
WWW: www.imd.ch
Contact: Mr. James Pulcrano
Description: Executive development programs for international general managers in global corporations.

Information Professionals Institute Seminars

3724 FM 1960 West, Suite 214
Houston, Texas 77068
Phone: (281) 537-8344
Fax: (281) 537-8332
Email: ipiseminars@burwellinc.com
WWW: www.burwellinc.com
Contact: Ms. Helen P. Burwell, Principal
Description: IPI Seminars offers regular and customized information research training to corporate executives and other professionals. Regular seminars include: operating a corporate information center; competitive intelligence; online and internet sources; comparative online searching and using public records for informed business decisions. Seminar leaders are recognized information exports and any of these programs can be customized to address specific corporate or industry needs.
Products/Services: Customized Information Research Seminars.

The Intellworks—Telemarketer Training & Phone Research

6213 Le Sage Avenue
Woodland Hills, California 91367-1327
Phone: (800) 975-1724 (818) 716-5030
Fax: (818) 991-5938
Email: inetlworks@earthlink.net
WWW: www.intellworks.com
Contact: Mr. Ronald La Vine
Description: Lead Qualification, Account Penetration.
Products/Services: PHONE TIPS for success Telemarketing Training.

THE Lett GROUP™
Teaching Professionals To Outclass Their Competition

The Lett Group

13116 Hutchinson Way, Suite 100
Silver Spring, Maryland 20906
Phone: (301) 946-8208
Fax: (301) 933-3884
Email: clett@lettgroup.com
WWW: www.lettgroup.com
Contact: Ms. Cynthia Lett, Director
Description: Outclass your competition! The Lett Group offers seminars, coaching and consultation for professionals at all levels of the corporate ladder in business etiquette. International protocol, communications skills and personal marketing. Let us design custom training programs, speak at your next meeting or work with individuals as personal coaches.
Products/Services: Seminars/coaching/private/corporate

Dr. Karen Otazo
241 North Plymouth Boulevard
Los Angeles, California 90004
Phone: (213) 469-0797
Fax: (213) 469-0791
Email: coach@hk.super.net
Contact: Dr. Karen L. Otazo
Description: Dr. Karen Otazo specializes in executive assessment and coaching using a highly personalized, confidential and innovative approach to developing executive effectiveness, especially cross-cultural.
Products/Services: Management Development, Coaching and Assessment.

Partners in Human Resources International, Inc.
9 East 37th Street, 9th Floor
New York, New York 10016
Phone: (212) 685-0400
Fax: (212) 726-9780
Email: partners@ingress.com
Contact: Ms. Linda Kline
Description: Human Resources Consulting firm (3 practice areas): Executive search, Organizational and Professional development, Outplacement and Executive coaching.

Peters & Associates, Inc.
5139 Green Braes E Drive
Indianapolis, Indiana 46234
Phone: (317) 299-4333
Fax: (317) 299-0993
Email: davidleep@aol.com
Contact: Mr. David L. Peters
Description: Innovation producing practices for research, development, manufacturing and marketing. Train innovation coaches; coach executives responsible for growth.
Products/Services: Innovation & Coaching.

Planasyst
9 Namoi Road
Northbridge, New South Wales 2063
Australia
Phone: 61 2 9958 2430
Contact: Mr. Gervace Pearce
Description: Strategy, Organizational Change and Leadership Development Consultants. Includes Business transformation and business Futures.
Products/Services: PlanAsyst Management Consulting.

Productivity Press
541 NE 20th Avenue
Portland, Oregon 97232-2862
Phone: (800) 394-6868x208 (503) 235-0600
WWW: www.ppress.com
Contact: Ms. Mary Pat Crum
Description: Productivity Press provides educational materials that support continuous improvement efforts in different industries but particularly for the manufacturing area. Concepts addressed: Just-In-Time, TPM, Mistake Proofing, Quick Changeover, SMED and many more.
Products/Services: Books, videos, learning packages.

Team Quality Development, Inc.
3354 Horrell Court
Fenton, Michigan 48430
Phone: (888) 629-4976
Fax: (810) 629-3206
Email: ajd@tqd.com
WWW: www.tqd.com
Contact: Mr. A. J. Deeds, President
Description: New audio CD: quality from the inside out- call us!

Speakers Bureaus/Agents

Business Communication Consultants, Inc.
P.O. Box 555
Billings, Montana 59103
Phone: (406) 248-4404
Fax: (406) 248-4404
Contact: Mr. Charles F. Tooley
Description: We provide speech training and engaging speakers for your meetings.
Products/Services: Executive Speaker Workshop.

The Marsee Group
P.O. Box 250
Davisburg, Michigan 48350
Phone: (248) 634-9821
Fax: (248) 634-8942
Contact: Mr. Bruce E. Marsee
Description: Why business intelligence is important in a global economy.
Products/Services: Business Intelligence.

PROFESSIONAL SERVICES

Professional Services

American Express
United Kingdom
Phone: 44 1273 863 863

American Express
Japan
Phone: 813 3220 6291

American Express
Federal Republic of Germany
Phone: 49 69 9797 1515

American Express Membership Rewards/Canada
Phone: (800) 668-2639

Compensation Advisors

Benefit Services Incorporated
36 Washington Street
Wellesley, Massachusetts 02181
Phone: (781) 237-3776
Fax: (781) 235-3907
Email: bsijohn@aol.com
Contact: Mr. John L. Coughlin
Description: Strategic employee benefit consulting for health & welfare plans for mid to large size employers.
Products/Services: Employee Benefit Consulting.

Benefits & Compensation Design Group
P.O. Box 369
Marlboro, New Jersey 07746-0369
Phone: (732) 972-1456
Fax: (732) 972-0214
Email: bencomp@s-wa.com
WWW: s-wa.com
Contact: Mr. John S. Sturges, CMC, PMC, SPWR, Managing Principal
Description: Design and implementation of cost-effective benefits, performance based compensation.
Products/Services: Human Resources Management Consultants.

Brennan, Thomsen Associates, Inc.
1819 Clarkson Road, Suite 305
Chesterfield, Missouri 63017-5071
Phone: (314) 530-1161
Fax: (314) 530-1109
Contact: Mr. E. James Brennan, President
Description: Competitive merit pay systems, reasonable executive compensation expert witness.
Products/Services: Direct pay consultants.

CR Compensation Resources, Inc.

Compensation Resources, Inc.
310 Route 17 North
Upper Saddle River, New Jersey 07458
Phone: (201) 934-0505
Fax: (201) 934-0737
WWW: www.compensationresources.com
Contact: Mr. Paul R. Dorf
Description: Compensation Resources, Inc. specializes in providing consulting in issues such as: Executive Compensation, Salary Administration, Sales Compensation, Performance Management, Market Pricing and Prevailing Wage Determination, Customized Salary Surveys, Litigation Support and other ancillary compensation issues. We work with mid-sized to large companies and have a library of over 1,600 surveys.

Diversified Human Resource Services
P.O. Box 115
Belcamp, Maryland 21017
Phone: (800) 459-0026 (410) 679-5555
Fax: (410) 679-4438
Email: dhrs@aol.com
Contact: Mr. Charles E. Scott, SPHR
Description: Compensation, work flow recommendations, job descriptions, Personnel Policy Manuals, Employee Handbooks, employee turnover reduction programs, absenteeism control. Reduce unemployment insurance rate, staff reduction planning, control Workers Compensation costs, Outplacement counseling, Executive Search, supervisory training, handle complaints from the Equal Employment Opportunity Commission, union contact negotiating, employee relations programs, employee newsletters, review of employee benefit programs such as vacations, sick leave, holidays, insurance, establish/review/ maintain your Human Resource System.
Products/Services: Human Resource Management Consulting.

Effective Compensation, Inc.
165 South Union Boulevard, Suite 516
Lakewood, Colorado 80228
Phone: (303) 980-0862
Fax: (303) 980-1087
Email: eci@eci-us.com
WWW: www.eci-us.com
Contact: Mr. Hoyt Doyel, President
Description: ECI helps clients nationally improve salary, incentive and equity programs.

H. L. Goehring & Associates, Inc.
3200 Wrenford Street
Dayton, Ohio 45409-1250
Phone: (937) 294-8854
Fax: (937) 294-4699
Contact: Mr. Hal Goehring, President
Description: Specialized consulting services in the management of human resources: executive search, organizational development, manpower planning, compensation plans, employee & labor relations, communications, profit and productivity improvement, mergers and acquisitions.
Products/Services: Senior level management consulting

Greenwood Consulting Services
P.O. Box 23171
Lansing, Michigan 48909-3171
Phone: (517) 332-6690 (517) 332-8927
Fax: (517) 332-9381
Email: whgIII@aol.com
Contact: Dr. William H. Greenwood, III, Ph.D.
Description: Assistance to all types of organizations in gainsharing implementation.
Products/Services: Gainsharing Programs.

John Jay & Company
100 Commercial Street, Suite 205
Portland, Maine 04101
Phone: (207) 772-6951
Fax: (207) 772-0159
Contact: Mr. Jay Hotchkiss, SPHR, CMC
Description: Human resources consulting firm offering wide range of services including compensation, employee relations and sexual harassment prevention.
Products/Services: Human Resources Consulting and Executive Search. Variable.

Management Solutions, Inc.
25 Pennsylvania Avenue
Reading, Massachusetts 01867
Phone: (781) 944-8168
Email: msinc@mediaone.net
Contact: Mr. Philip Sanborn
Description: HRPRO—Information technology "tool" designed to automate the function.
Products/Services: Organizational Dynamics/Development, Compensation Management, HRPRO(tm).

Steven D. Norton
1209 East Wayne Street North
South Bend, Indiana 46615
Phone: (219) 234-3358
Fax: (219) 234-3358
Email: snorton@lusp.edu
Contact: Dr. Steve D. Norton
Description: Development and implementation of AC and PA systems.
Products/Services: Assessment Centers & Performance Appraisal.

Olney Associates Inc.
15 Broad Street, Suite 612
Boston, Massachusetts 02109
Phone: (617) 227-1642
Fax: (617) 227-6626
Contact: Ms. Brenda Curley
Description: Compensation program design, performance management, salary administration, compensation/benefit surveys.

Organization Consultants, Inc.
1909 Charlotte Drive
Charlotte, North Carolina 28203
Phone: (704) 375-6262
Fax: (704) 375-1118
Contact: Mr. Glenn B. Williams

Rhodeback & Associates
202 Pine Willow Court
Friendswood, Texas 77546
Phone: (281) 482-8924
Contact: Ms. Melanie J. Rhodeback, Ed.D.
Description: Compensation Consulting; Measurement and Statistical Consulting; Specialists in applying MSMT & Statistics to management decisions with applications in survey design instrument validation; attitude and opinion assessments.
Products/Services: Compensation/Applied Research for Business.

Robert L. Sauer Associates
5650 Elderberry Road
Noblesville, Indiana 46060-9708
Phone: (317) 776-2109
Email: rsauer5650@aol.com
Contact: Mr. Robert L. Sauer
Description: Base and/or incentives sweepers to CEOs; all organizations.
Products/Services: Compensation & Organization Planning.

Sbarra & Company, Inc.
P.O. Box 124
Lyndonville, Vermont 05851
Phone: (802) 626-3376
Email: bobsbarra@kingcon.com
Contact: Mr. Robert A. Sbarra
Description: Design base and incentive pay programs for all employee groups.

Michael H. Schuster
85 North Cliff Drive
Narragansett, Rhode Island 02882-1910
Phone: (401) 789-3498
Fax: (401) 789-3525
Email: schustr9-2@idt.net
WWW: www.chrs.net
Contact: Mr. Michael H. Schuster
Description: Human resources compensation, and growth strategies for a changing world.
Products/Services: Competitive Human Resources Strategies, LLC (CHRS).

John Steiger Financial Services
699 Boylston Street, Suite 500
Boston, Massachusetts 02116
Phone: (617) 262-2500
Fax: (617) 262-1652
Contact: Mr. John Steiger
Description: Specializing in working with consultants: professional business succession planning, employee benefits and retirement plans, executive compensation plans, professional estate and financial planning.

Lee Stephens & Associates
2168 Balboa Avenue, Suite 3
San Diego, California 92109
Phone: (619) 270-8800
Email: augustpat@aol.com
Contact: Mr. Lee Stephens

Synapse Human Resource Consulting Group
5956 Sherry Lane, Suite 1000
Sherry Lane Place
Dallas, Texas 75225
Phone: (214) 691-3939
Email: synapsecon@aol.com
Contact: Mr. Michael Schwartz
Description: Retained Executive Search, Compensation Consulting, Organizational Development, Employee Relations and Communications, Training and Development.
Products/Services: Human Resource Consulting.

Triad Consultants, Inc.
175 Olde Half Day Road
Lincolnshire, Illinois 60069
Phone: (847) 634-8300
Fax: (847) 821-7360
Email: triadcons@aol.com
Contact: Mr. Douglas M. Cravens
Description: Design and installation of incentive and salary management systems.

Walden Personnel Testing
4115 Sherbrooke Lane, Room 100
Montreal, Quebec H3Z 3C5
Canada
Phone: (514) 989-9555
Fax: (514) 989-9934
Email: tests@waldentesting.com
WWW: waldentesting.com
Contact: Mr. Stephen Silver
Description: Pre-employment skills testing.
Products/Services: Personnel testing, consulting, test development & validation.

WMS & Company Inc.
20128 Valley Forge Circle
King of Prussia, Pennsylvania 19406
Phone: (610) 783-7733
Fax: (610) 783-6591
Email: wmsandco@erols.com
WWW: expert-market.com/wms
Contact: Mr. Robert J. Sahl
Description: Consultation in compensation planning and the applied behavioral sciences.
Products/Services: Equi-Comp(c).

Export Advisors

ASECOSA
Travessera De Gracia, 13 5-4
Barcelona, 08021
Spain
Phone: 34 93 414 66 08
Fax: 34 93 414 00 14
Email: asecosa@mx2.redestb.es
Contact: Mr. Jose-Luis Terricabras
Description: "Market entry": to provide support to companies interested in Spanish market"Competitive knowledge": to provide any type of information about Spain and Spanish market.
Products/Services: "Market entry" and "Competitive knowledge".

Camp, Inc.
4600 Prospect Avenue
Cleveland, Ohio 44302
Phone: (800) NOW-CAMP (216) 432-5369
Fax: (216) 361-2900
WWW: www.camp.org
Contact: Mr. Joel C. Anyim
Description: CAMP, Inc. assists manufacturers to be more profitable and productive through modernization projects, business management practices, advanced manufacturing, information technology, and human resource & workforce development.
Products/Services: Manufacturing Solutions.

General Management Services Inc.
76 Mamaroneck Avenue, #6
White Plains, New York 10601
Phone: (914) 946-2734
Fax: (914) 946-3093
Email: gmspub@aol.com
WWW: centretrade.com
Contact: Mr. Warren Hastongs
Description: Full international trade consulting for export trade, logistics and finance.
Products/Services: International Trade Consulting.

GOIC
P.O. Box 5114
60, Corniche, West Bay
Doha,
State of Qatar
Phone: 974 858 802
Fax: 974 831 465
Email: goic@goic.org.qa
WWW: www.goic@goic.org.qa
Contact: Dr. Abdulrahman A. Al-Jafary
Products/Services: Industrial Consultancy, Research firm, books/directories, magazines/newsletters.

Impact Business Startup
Orionstrasse 6
Unterschleissheim
Munich, D-85716
Federal Republic of Germany
Phone: 49 89 3104020
Fax: 49 89 3104021
Email: info@impact-bs.com
WWW: www.impact-bs.com
Contact: Ms. Brigitte Krenn
Description: We offer a comprehensive service in establishing branches/subsidiaries for companies that want to expand their business to Munich Germany.

Interdevelopment Oy
Topeliuksenkatu 35 A 33
Helsinki, FIN-00250
Finland
Phone: 358 9 2412557
Fax: 358 9 2412558
Email: reino.routamo@interd.pp.fi
WWW: www.interdevelopment.fi
Contact: Mr. Reino Routamo, Managing Director
Description: Interdevelopment Oy is an internationally operative, virtual management consulting and market-development company. Our headquarters are on the Web:<www.interdevelopment.fi> and our physical offices are in Austria, Estonia, Finland, Germany, Luxembourg, and Sweden. We are specialized in assisting our clients to enter the European markets. We offer market studies, assistance in marketing planning and M&A, and market monitoring, also in cooperation with other consulting firms. Members of LJK/FEACO.
Products/Services: DFO - Developing Foreign Operations.

MJL International, Inc.
15237 Sunset Boulevard, Suite 123
Pacific Palisades, California 90272
Phone: (310) 573-9659
Fax: (310) 573-9609
Email: mjlinternational@worldnet.att.net
WWW: home.att.net/mjlinternational/
Contact: Mr. Michael J. Labriola
Description: Foreign business development, foreign market research, foreign investigations.
Products/Services: Global Business Consultants.

The PRS Group
6320 Fly Road, Suite 102
East Syracuse, New York 13057-0248
Phone: (315) 829-3748 (315) 431-0511
Fax: (315) 431-0200
Email: custserv@prsgoup.com
WWW: www.prsgroup.com
Contact: Mr. Tom Gerken
Description: International country information. Two risk services monitor, analyze and forecast the political, economic and financial risk of international business in 144 countries. Market newsletters provide international demographic and consumer information.
Products/Services: Country Information Reports available in paper, CD-ROM and Online.

Insurance

Agency Marketing Services
P.O. Box 41786
St. Petersburg, Florida 33743
Phone: (813) 384-1036
Fax: (813) 343-4123
Contact: Ms. Donna Roberts
Description: Provide E & O insurance to the consulting industry in Florida

CYMRU Insurance Service
P.O. Box 472080
San Francisco, California 94147-2080
Phone: (888) 441-2587 (415) 441-2587
Fax: (415) 928-1179
Email: cymruins@aol.com
WWW: ezone.com/bis
Contact: Ms. Joanne Lochtefeld
Description: Professional liability, Errors & Omission, General liability, Workers-compensation for the computer & management industries.
Products/Services: Liability, General, E&O.

Executive Office Assistance
1253 Worcester Road, Suite 302
Framingham, Massachusetts 01701-5250
Phone: (508) 879-7071
Fax: (508) 626-9034
Email: ncbeoa@aol.com
Contact: Ms. Nancy Boynton
Description: Office Space/shared secretarial services/word processing, telephone answering/voice mail.

The Finsure House Inc.
5302-E. Memorial Drive, #1407
Stone Mountain, Georgia 30083
Phone: (404) 297-1952
Fax: (404) 298-9028
Email: finsureh@avana.net
WWW: membro.tripod.com/finsearch/index.html
Contact: Mr. G. Waterhouse
Description: International insurance and reinsurance managing general agency.
Products/Services: International insurance & reinsurance.

Jardine Group Services Corporation
48 Cornell Road
Latham, New York 12110
Phone: (800) 998-5545
Fax: (518) 782-3051
Email: jbradley@jgsc.com
WWW: www.jgsc.com/mcpl/
Contact: Mr. Jim Bradley
Description: Consultants professional liability/malpractice insurance protection.
Products/Services: CE & O Consultants Errors & Omissions.

Katzman Insurance Agency

10 Prince Street
Monticello, New York 12701
Phone: (800) 967-5252
Fax: (914) 328-4351
Email: katzmanins@msn.com
Contact: Mr. Jack Katzman
Description: Errors & omissions insurance, general liability, property, workers compensation, business auto, umbrella and bonding. Program coordinator for 5 national consulting associations and 1 group affiliation program.

National Insurance Professionals Corporation

1040 NE Hostmark Street, #200
Poulsbo, Washington 98370-8720
Phone: (360) 697-3611
Fax: (360) 697-3688
WWW: www.nipc.com
Contact: Mr. Barry Clipsham

Interpretors & Translators

Grace & St. Peter's Chinese Language School
524 Anneslie Road
Baltimore, Maryland 21212-2009
Phone: (410) 377-8143
Contact: Ms. Lillian Lee

Diana Jovanovic
1008 Hobbs Drive
Colesville, Maryland 20904
Phone: (301) 384-5138
Email: djovan6291@aol.com
Description: Conferences, seminars on VIPs.
Products/Services: Portuguese & Spanish interpreters. Voice overs teachers.

Shifra Kilov
251 River Road
Millington, New Jersey 07946
Phone: (908) 647-8163
Fax: (908) 647-8163
Email: shifrak@aol.com
Contact: Mr. Shifra Kilov
Description: Business, legal, technical, medical, translations and interpretations (Russian and Latvian).

Hisako Sato MacQueen
9300 Chanute Drive
Bethesda, Maryland 20814
Phone: (301) 493-0091
Fax: (301) 564-1493
Email: 71500.2667@compuserve.com
Description: Simultaneous or consecutive interpreting from/to English/Japanese for international conferences, seminars, business meetings, etc.
Products/Services: Japanese-English language services of Washington.

Russign Servicco
3216 Abell Avenue
Baltimore, Maryland 21218
Phone: (410) 467-3308
Fax: (410) 467-3308
Email: sjfrank@clark.net
Contact: Mr. Stephen J. Frank, Owner/Proprietor
Description: Russian language interpretation/translation and American sign language interpretation/transliteration.
Products/Services: Interpreters and translators.

Sokolov Yelena
7116 Winter Rose Path
Columbia, Maryland 21045
Phone: (410) 381-1653
Description: Russian-English; English-Russian, Ukranian.

Randall T. Wert
159 Church Hill Road
Lenhartsville, Pennsylvania 19534-9318
Phone: (800) 437-6261 (610) 756-4380
Email: rtwert@fast.net
Contact: Mr. Randall T. Wert
Description: Precise English translations of German documents from all technical fields. Fast, free quotes of price and turnaround time.
Products/Services: German to English Translations.

Suzanne M. Zeng
1427 Alexander Street, #207
Honolulu, Hawaii 96822
Phone: (808) 956-4421 (808) 942-3683
Contact: Ms. Suzanne Zeng
Description: Handle translation and interpretation needs for many languages, especially Asian languages. Help coordinate conference and other interpretation needs.
Products/Services: Translation & Interpreting Services and Management.

Mergers & Acquisitions Brokers

Acquest International L.P.
1760 Market Street, 12th Floor
Philadelphia, Pennsylvania 19103
Phone: (215) 496-4500
Fax: (215) 496-4501
Email: acquest2@aol.com
Contact: Mr. Peter Kuhlman
Description: M&A advisory services—conducting sales of companies, performing acquisition searches for buyers, negotiating recapitalizations, rendering fairness opinions and valuations.

De Bellas & Company
2 Northpoint Drive, Suite 230
Houston, Texas 77060
Phone: (281) 448-5252
Fax: (281) 448-5264
Email: rick@debellas.com
WWW: www.debellas.com
Contact: Mr. Richard G. Wilson, Jr.
Description: De Bellas & Co. is the leading investment banking firm providing merger, acquisition and financial advisory services to staffing and information technology services businesses and professional employer service organizations..
Products/Services: Investment Banking Firm.

Lyons & Associates
15R Hartford Avenue, Suite 2A-D
Granby, Connecticut 06035
Phone: (860) 653-4770
Fax: (860) 653-4263
Email: jlyons10@tiac.net
WWW: www.lyons-assoc.com
Contact: Mr. Jack Lyons
Description: M+A Services to the staffing services and information technology services industries.
Products/Services: Mergers & Acquisitions Brokers.

O'Conor, Wright Wyman, Inc.
211 Congress Street, 9th Floor
Boston, Massachusetts 02110
Phone: (617) 482-8330
Fax: (617) 482-8236
Email: fanklinw@aol.com
Contact: Mr. Frank Wyman, Chairman
Description: Identify buyers for selling clients and sellers for buying clients.
Products/Services: Corporate Finance.

Siebrand-Wilton Associates, Inc.
P.O. Box 2498
New York, New York 10008-2498
Phone: (212) 353-2525
Email: swa@s-wa.com
Contact: Mr. J.S. Sturges, President
Description: Assess, plan and implement human resources aspects of mergers/acquisitions.
Products/Services: Merger and acquisition consulting.

Practice Management Advisors

Battelle
P.O. Box 5395
4000 NE 41st Street
Seattle, Washington 98105
Phone: (206) 528-3272 (206) 361-1980
Fax: (206) 528-3554
Email: macaulay@battelle.org
WWW: www.seattle.battelle.org/services/oe/
Contact: Dr. Jennifer Macaulay
Description: I can assist you in designing and implementing change initiatives to improve the short-term and long-term success of your organization. Organizational assessment, strategic planning, change management, training.
Products/Services: Organizational Improvement Consulting.

Robert Bennett Associates
P.O. Box 261
Little Neck, New York 11363
Phone: (212) 949-2355 (718) 428-5455
Contact: Ms. Mary Bloom
Products/Services: Attorneys in all Categories.

Blaiklock Consulting
6668 Raintree Road
Roanoke, Virginia 24018
Phone: (540) 989-5785 (540) 772-9500
Email: blaikloc@rbnet.com
WWW: www.ibt.net/blaiklock/
Contact: Mr. Paul Blaiklock
Description: Consulting on marketing technology-based products to the industrial and commercial markets; specialization in automation systems.
Products/Services: Technology product marketing.

Gardner Carton & Douglas

321 North Clark Street, Suite 3400
Chicago, Illinois 60610-4795
Phone: (312) 245-8841
Fax: (312) 644-3381
Contact: Mr. Alex W. Zabrosky
Description: General counsel to consultancies, including organizational matters, client contracts, employment law matters, malpractice and collection litigation, intellectual property, strategic alliances and restructuring, mergers and acquisitions, government contracts, international expansion.
Products/Services: Legal services to consulting firms

The Hawver Group

Two Research Way
Princeton, New Jersey 08540-6628
Phone: (609) 987-8001
Fax: (609) 987-8055
Email: Hawvergrp@aol.com
Contact: Dr. Dennis A. Hawver, CMC, President
Description: Management/organizational and organizations maximize their opportunities.
Products/Services: Executive, Organizational Improvement and Management Development Consulting.

Gardner, Carton & Douglas

Consultancy Law Practice Group

Attorneys specializing in serving the consulting profession

Alex W. Zabrosky
321 North Clark Street
Suite 3400, Quaker Tower
Chicago, Illinois 60610
(312) 245-8841

1301 K Street, N.W.
Suite 900, East Tower
Washington D.C. 20005
(202) 408-7100

Klemm & Associates
2400 Cripple Creek Drive
St. Louis, Missouri 63129-5039
Phone: (314) 846-2440
Fax: (314) 846-2440
Contact: Mr. Andy Klemm
Description: Help when you need to make values clear, conceive strategy soundly, change the way you do things, give people accountabilities, and provide rewards for achievers. Making organizations stronger by transferring knowledge and skill. Consulting with executives on values, strategy, working through change, development of people, teams, productivity, compensation, and surveys.
Products/Services: General Management Consulting - Consulting to Consultants.

Maister Associates
P.O. Box 946
Boston, Massachusetts 02117
Phone: (617) 262-5968
Fax: (617) 262-7907
WWW: www.davidmaister.com
Contact: Mr. David Maister, Director of Marketing

Nexus Consultants to Management
P.O. Box 1531
Novato, California 94948
Phone: (415) 897-4400
Fax: (415) 898-2252
Email: jimnexus@aol.com
Contact: Dr. J. H. Carbone
Description: NEXUS is a strategic management consulting proprietorship serving more than 100 large (NYSE) and small clients since 1962; advising boards, owners, and CEOs nationally from California. NEXUS is in the innovative solutions business, specializing in intractable client opportunities; helping teams resolve mission, values, vision, culture, strategic goals, organization design, grand strategy, strategic planning; analyzing competition, demystifying internal and external environments; leading strategic and functional planning teams, applying revealed grand strategy; producing efficient-productive systems and processes using system analysis- and efficient-productive managers using executive advising, coaching.
Products/Services: Managerial Consulting.

Organization Transitions, Inc.
75 Huguenot Drive
East Greenwich, Rhode Island 02818
Phone: (401) 884-4195
Contact: Mr. Anthony DiBella
Description: Consultants in organization development, team and organizational learning.
Products/Services: Organization learning inventory.

Personnel Decisions
600 Las Colinas Boulevard East, #1700
Irving, Texas 75039
Phone: (972) 401-8104 (817) 329-8448
Fax: (972) 401-3193
Email: tomj@pdi-corp.com
WWW: www.pdi-corp.com
Contact: Mr. Tom Janz
Products/Services: Selection Systems.

Sherwood Partners, Inc.

1849 Sawtelle Boulevard, Suite 543
Los Angeles, California 90025
Phone: (310) 477-8990 ext 21
Fax: (310) 477-8402
Email: mdp@shrwood.com
WWW: shrwood.com
Contact: Mr. Martin Pichinson
Description: Sherwood Advisors, LLP is a full service advisory firm that solves companies' problems in the areas of finance, operations, emerging growth and strategic partnering. Each member of our staff has experience in assisting troubled and growing companies. We also help companies establish a presence in Mexico and Mexican companies enter the US market.
Products/Services: Finance, Operations, Workouts, Crisis Management.

SHERWOOD PARTNERS, Inc.

1849 Sawtelle Boulevard, Suite 543
Los Angeles, CA 90025
Tel: 310.477.8990 Fax: 310.477.8402
email: mdp@shrwood.com
Visit us at www.sherwood.com

SERVICES

- FINANCING & DEBT RESTRUCTURING
- CORPORATE CRISIS & TURNAROUND
- OPERATION PROBLEMS
- GROWTH ISSUES
- RECEIVABLE MANAGEMENT
- CORPORATE RESTRUCTURING
- COURT RECEIVERSHIPS
- STRATEGIC PARTNERSHIPS
- RELATIONSHIPS & ALLIANCES IN MEXICO

PUBLICATIONS

Publications

Forbes
CUSTOM PUBLISHING

Forbes Custom Publishing
85 Fifth Avenue
New York, New York 10003
Phone: (800) 242-8786
Fax: (212) 367-4876
Email: fcpinfo@forbes.com
Description: At Forbes Custom Publishing, a division of Forbes, Inc., we manage books from concept through manufacturing, to warehousing and marketing. Our editors will design professional books and materials for your employees, members or workshop participants while maximizing your potential income.

Books/Directories

Alpha Publications
c/o Kennedy Information
One Kennedy Place, Route 12 South
Fitzwilliam, NH 03447
Phone: (800) 531-0007
Fax: (603) 585-9555
Email: bookstore@kennedyinfo.com
WWW: www.kennedyinfo.com
Contact: Customer service
Description: Regional consulting reports include: *Management Consultancy Services in Hong Kong; Management Consultancy Services in Japan; Management Consultancy Services in Western Europe; Management Consultancy Services in the United States.* Call for further information and prices.

Burwell Enterprises, Inc.
3724 FM 1960 West, #214
Houston, Texas 77068
Phone: (281) 537-9051
Fax: (281) 537-8332
Email: burwellinfo@burwellinc.com
WWW: www.burwellinc.com
Contact: Ms. Helen P. Burwell
Description: BE publishes "The Burwell World Directory of Information Brokers", an annual directory designed to link those who need information with the companies and experts who can find it anywhere in the world. BE also produces several other publications, such as the bi-monthly "Information Broker" newsletter, which provides business and legal advice and counsel for the Independent information research consultant.
Products/Services: Burwell World Directory of Information Brokers, 13th edition.

The Corporate Directory of U.S. Public Companies
Walker's Research, LLC
1650 Borel Place, Suite 130
San Mateo, California 94402
Phone: (800) 258-5737 (650) 341-1110
Fax: (650) 341-2351
Email: walkersres@aol.com
Contact: Ms. Barbara Delmar
Description: Summary business and financial information on all of the 10,000 publicly traded companies in the United States, including officers, Directors, 5% owners and stock information. Eight indexes. User-friendly CD-ROM search software facilitates combination searches, data manipulation, mailing labels and export to user database.

The Directory of Management Consultants
Kennedy Information LLC
One Kennedy Place, Route 12 South
Fitzwilliam, New Hampshire 03447
Phone: (800) 531-0007
Fax: (603) 585-9555
Email: bookstore@kennedyinfo.com
WWW: www.kennedyinfo.com
Description: Reliable, up-to-date information from the publishers of the industry's prime source of news and advice, *Consultants News*. The profiles of over 1,800 management consulting firms, with fresh data on each firm, include paragraph descriptions followed by billing and staff-size ranges. The directory has four indexes: services offered, industries served, locations, and over 7,100 key principals with firm affiliations. Introductory material includes over 30 pages on consulting associations and selecting and working with consulting professionals.

Disaster Recovery Yellow Pages
25 Ellison Road
Newton, Massachusetts 02159
Phone: (617) 332-3496
Fax: (617) 332-4358
Contact: Mr. Steven Lewis
Description: A unique listing of over 3000 disaster-recovery vendors, divided into over 255 different categories, ranging from emergency replacement equipment suppliers, to smoke-odor counteracting services to trauma counselors, microfilm dryers, etc.
Products/Services: Disaster Recovery Yellow Pages.

Gale Research
835 Penobscot Building
Detroit, Michigan 48226
Phone: (800) 347-4253 (313) 961-2242
Fax: (313) 961-6815
WWW: www.gale.com
Contact: Ms. Jennifer Mast
Description: Lists approximately 30,000 publications, online sources, associations, and research centers that cover business- and industry - related issues. The directory is arranged by subject terms (i.e., name of industry, business issue, management concept, or workplace issue), so users can readily pinpoint the resources that pertain to their information needs. Also contains an alphabetical listing of all the resources covered in the book.
Products/Services: The Encyclopedia of Business Information Sources.

Goal/QPC
13 Branch Street
Methuen, Massachusetts 01844-1953
Phone: (800) 643-4316 (978) 685-3900
Fax: (978) 685-6151
Email: service@goal.com
WWW: www.goalqpc.com
Contact: Ms. Dorie L. Overhoff
Description: Improving everyone's daily work and business processes through practical products.
Products/Services: Memory Jogger System™ System of pocket guides and products.

Jossey-Bass/Pfeiffer
350 Sansome Street
San Francisco, California 94104
Phone: (415) 782-3227
Fax: (415) 433-1711
Email: mholt@jbp.com
WWW: www.pfeiffer.com
Contact: Mr. Matthew Holt, Editor
Description: Publisher of HRD material for consultants, trainers and managers.
Products/Services: HRD Resources

Kalorama Information
7200 Wisconsin Avenue
Bethesda, Maryland 20814
Phone: (301) 961-6734
Fax: (301) 961-6790
Email: rob@csa.com
WWW: findexonline.com
Contact: Mr. Robert Granader
Description: Worldwide directory of market research reports. Over 3,000 new reports.
Products/Services: Findex: The Directory of Market Research Reports, Studies, and Surveys.

Kennedy's Directory of Venture Capital Firms

Kennedy Information LLC
One Kennedy Place, Route 12 South
Fitzwilliam, New Hampshire 03447
Phone: (800) 531-0007
Fax: (603) 585-9555
Email: bookstore@kennedyinfo.com
WWW: www.kennedyinfo.com
Description: Detailed listings of 869 venture capital funds include full contact data, industry specialties, key principals, fund sizes, financing activities, and much more. Includes introductory articles by industry experts and an industries index to match firms with specific projects.

Thomas Register of American Manufacturers

5 Penn Plaza
New York, New York 10001
Phone: (800) 699-9822 (212) 290-7323
Fax: (212) 290-7335
Email: ordertr@thomasregister.com
WWW: www.thomasregister.com
Contact: Ms. Alisa Fogel
Description: Published annually, Thomas Register of American Manufacturers is by far the most complete and helpful specifying and buying guide published today. It provides "instant" sourcing information on nearly 56,000 industrial products and services, along with comprehensive specifications and availability information from thousands of manufacturers.
Products/Services: Thomas Register of American Manufacturers.

Velocity Business Publishing, Inc.

15 Main Street
Bristol, Vermont 05443
Phone: (802) 453-6669 (802) 453-2164
Email: action@agilemanager.com
WWW: www.agilemanager.com
Contact: Mr. Jeff Olson, Publisher
Description: We publish books and software on high-leverage business topics.
Products/Services: Agile Manager Series

Magazines/Newsletters

Consultants News

Kennedy Information LLC
One Kennedy Place, Route 12 South
Fitzwilliam, New Hampshire 03447
Phone: (800) 531-0007
Email: subscribe@kennedyinfo.com
WWW: www.kennedyinfo.com

Description: *Consultants News* is the authoritative voice of the consulting industry, covering news, analysis, practice advice, proprietary data and opinion since 1970. Here's the information successful consultants need to stay ahead of the pack. Regular features include *profiles* of innovative firms, large and small, with the financial data that gives you the real story, from top management to bottom line . . . *statistics* on the changing size and shape of consulting today, including the *CN 50*—an annual ranking of the 50 largest firms with sector and regional analyses, M&A activity and more . . . *issues and trends* that affect your practice, including commentary by leading observers of the profession . . . *best practices* that can lead you to profitable new opportunities, including emerging practice areas, new services and more . . . plus frank discussions on how firms deal with tough ethical and business issues. Published monthly, 12pp./issue.

Products/Services: *The Directory of Management Consultants;* proprietary research reports from Kennedy Information Research Group (KIRG) including the *Global Human Resources Management Consulting Marketplace, MBA Recruiting: Gaining a Competitive Edge, Electronic Commerce Consulting* and others; CN "Best Practices" conferences and seminars; the Consultant's Bookstore; *Consulting* magazine; *The CN Career Guide; The Consultants ResourceBook;* KIRG consulting services; and more.

PUBLICATIONS • MAGAZINES/NEWSLETTERS

The Journal of Management Consulting, Inc.
858 Longview Road
Burlingame, California 94010-6974
Phone: (800) 568-5668 (650) 342-1954
Fax: (650) 344-5005
Email: jmc@jmcforum.com
WWW: www.jmcforum.com
Contact: Mr. E. Michael Shays, CMC, FIMC
Description: A semi-annual professional journal for management consultants about management consulting practice and process. JMC collects and publishes the special body of knowledge of this profession. See our advertisement.
Products/Services: The Journal of Management Consulting, article reprints, compact disk of the first 15 years.

Build Your Own Consulting Library: Fifteen Years of the

Journal of Management Consulting

Over 400 timeless articles on the profession of management consulting from our 1st issue in 1982 to our 36th in 1997. USD $195.00

This CD contains 2000 pages in Adobe PDF format. Text items are full-text searchable. Graphics, including charts, graphs and pictures are captured in image format. All PDF files are indexed by title and author. The CD includes Adobe Reader 3.0 software for Windows and Macintosh platforms.

THE JOURNAL OF MANAGEMENT CONSULTING, INC.
858 Longview Road, Burlingame, CA 94010-6974 USA
Tel: 650 342 1954 • Fax: 650 344 5005
Email: jmc@jmcforum.com • http://www.jmcforum.com

PCM Consulting Group
152 Morristown Road, Suite 1
Matawan, New Jersey 07747
Phone: (732) 441-1833 (732) 441-0102
Fax: (732) 441-0511
Email: sandy@pcmreport.com
WWW: www.pcmreport.com
Contact: Ms. Sandy Bashover
Description: Consultant for long distance phone service and prepaid phone cards. Publishers of PCM Report Magazine.

Zweig White & Associates, Inc.
One Apple Hill, Box 8325
Natick, Massachusetts 01760
Phone: (508) 651-1559
WWW: www.zwa.com
Contact: Mr. Mark C. Zweig
Description: Full service management consultants and publishers of management information for the A/E/P and environmental consulting industries.

RESEARCH

Research

Kennedy Information Research Group
KIRG
Kennedy Information LLC
One Kennedy Place, Route 12 South
Fitzwilliam, New Hampshire 03447
Phone: (800) 531-0007 (603) 585-3101
Fax: (603) 585-6401
WWW: www.kennedyinfo.com
Contact: Mr. Tim Bourgeois
Description: Kennedy Information Research Group provides objective worldwide market intelligence on the management consulting profession. Based on surveys and interviews with current, potential and past clients and consultants, research and analysis is delivered through syndicated and custom reports. KIRG also accesses its proprietary database, which contains detailed information on 2000+ management consulting firms, and library, providing the most extensive coverage of consulting in the world. Contact KIRG for more information on special reports and customized research..
Products/Services: Kennedy Information Research Group.

Compensation & Recruiting Trends in Management Consulting
A new research report for consultants from Kennedy Information Research Group

- **Lower** employee turnover
- **Boost** key employee morale
- **Expand** your candidate pool
- **Improve** your cost-per-hire ratio
- **Increase** acceptance of your firm's offers
- and much more...

Compensation & Recruiting Trends in Management Consulting: $995

Whether you're looking to grow your practice or work smarter with what you have, here's the analysis you need to compete in today's increasingly crowded consulting market.

Whether you're a Big Five behemoth with an appetite for thousands or a solo thinking of adding your first analyst – whether you're looking for seasoned veterans or new college graduates – there are simply not enough talented people out there.

But the numbers can add up for your firm if you have the right intelligence and analysis. Compensation & Recruiting Trends in Management Consulting provides the hard data you need to retain and attract talent so you can spend more time generating business and serving clients.

KENNEDY INFORMATION RESEARCH GROUP
One Kennedy Place • Fitzwilliam, NH 03447 • 800-531-0007

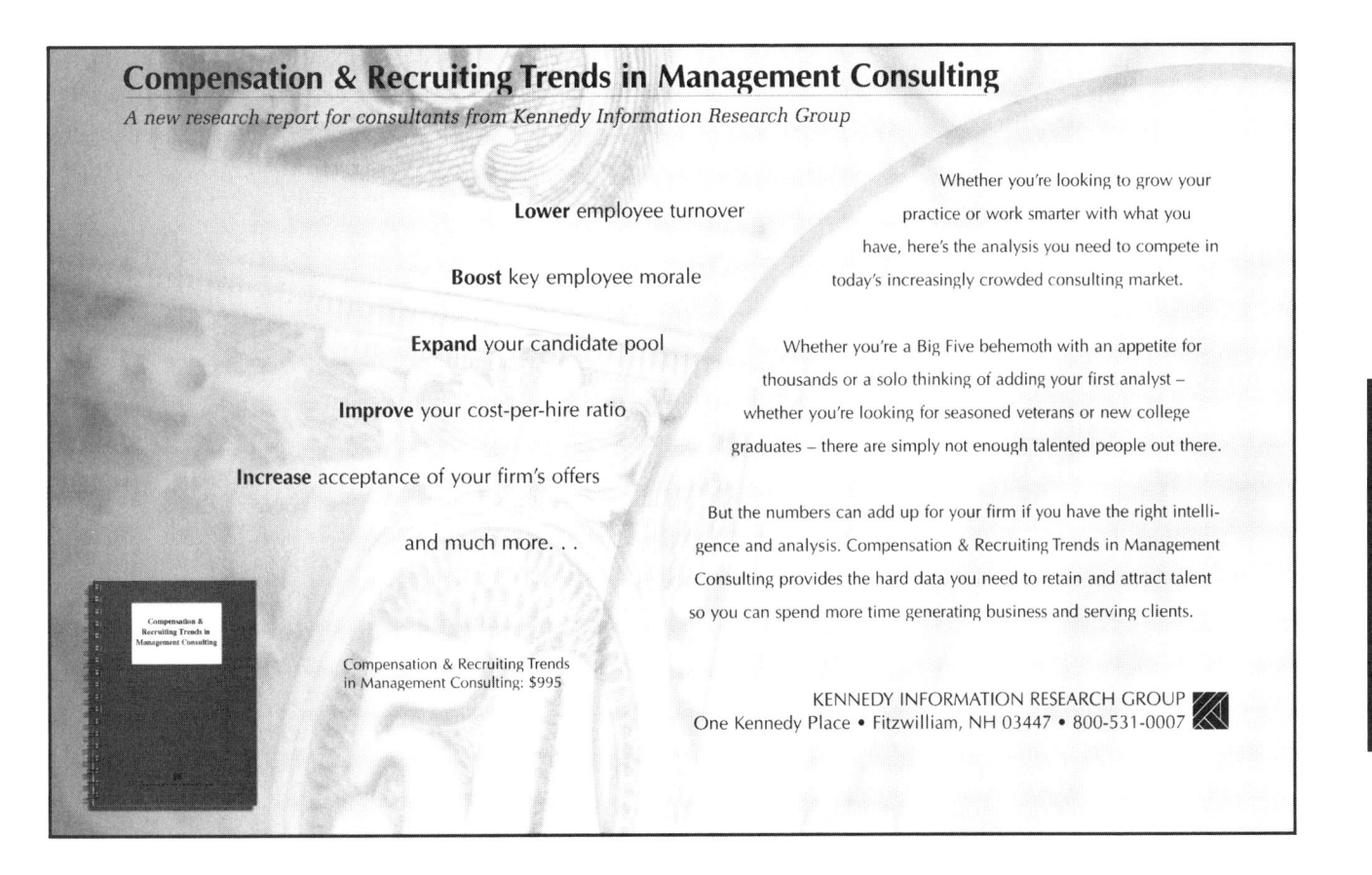

Research Databases

Bureau Van Dijk Netherlands
Jan Luijkenstraat 94
Amsterdam, NL 1071
Netherlands
Phone: 31 20 6719926
Fax: 31 20 6720951
Email: cdrom@euronet.nl
WWW: www.bvdep.com
Contact: Mr. Erik-Jan Van Kleef
Description: Bureau van Dijk specializes in financial databases and analysis tools and cooperates with the world's best data providers to guarantee the highest standard of data. Products are available on CD-ROM or as Internet/Intranet applications. Bureau van Dijk's headquarters are based in Brussels, Belgium. Bureau van Dijk maintains other offices in New York, Germany, Italy, Japan, Austria, Denmark, Netherlands, United Kingdom and Singapore.
Products/Services: Amadeus, Bankscope, Direct, Global Researcher, Reach and a variety of regional focused databases (e.g. Japan, Belgium, UK, Germany, etc.).

Claritas, Inc.
1525 Wilson Boulevard, Suite 1000
Arlington, Virginia 22209
Phone: (800) 284-4868
Fax: (703) 812-2701
Email: info@claritas.com
WWW: www.claritas.com
Contact: Mr. Brent Roderick
Description: Demographic reports available on the Internet for business strategy.
Products/Services: Claritas Connect on the Internet

Corporate Technology Information Services
12 Alfred Street, Suite 200
Woburn, Massachusetts 01801-1915
Phone: (800) 333-8036 (781) 932-3939
Fax: (781) 932-6335
Email: sales@corptech.com
WWW: www.corptech.com
Contact: Mr. Steven Parker
Description: CorpTech provides accurate company profiles on 50,000+ high-tech manufacturers and developers and names, titles and responsibilities of 200,000+ senior executives. 3,000 detailed codes allow you to search for companies in a way not possible with SIC codes. 80% of the database consists of privately held companies or operating units of larger companies. Company profiles include over 20 different data points plus a resume of corporate change over the past 10 years.
Products/Services: CorpTech.

International Market Research Information (IMRI)
70 London Road
Coalville, Leicestershire LE67 3AJ
United Kingdom
Phone: 44 1530 510 718
Fax: 44 1509 891 080
Email: IMRI@clara.net
WWW: www.IMRIresearch.com
Description: All sources of market research information on DataStar, Dialog, Hard-copy.
Products/Services: IMRI Database

The Investext Group
22 Thomson Place
Boston, Massachusetts 02210
Phone: (800) 662-7878 (617) 345-2704
Fax: (617) 330-1986
Email: webber@tfn.com
WWW: www.investext.com
Contact: Mr. John Webber
Description: The Investext Group is the world's leading provider of in-depth business research and analysis, offering the largest electronic collection of investment, market and trade association research.
Products/Services: Research Bank Web™.

Library Technology Alliance, Ltd.
P.O. Box 77232
Washington, District of Columbia 20013-8232
Phone: (202) 789-2099
Fax: (202) 789-2474
Email: lta@bellatlantic.com
WWW: www.periodicals.net
Contact: Ms. Nuchine Nobari
Description: Books and Periodicals ONLINE database offers quick and convenient access to online research. This comprehensive source identifies newspapers, periodicals, wire services, newsletters and reference works that can be found online. Arranged alphabetically, each entry has title, ISSN, online services that host the publication, URL address, dates of coverage when available and whether the coverage format is index, abstract and, if available, in full text. Books and Periodicals ONLINE is also available on CD-ROM and in print. The electronic format can be delivered in ascii, comma delimited, InMagic or in dbf format.

Market IQ, Inc.
740 River Road, Suite 210
Fair Haven, New Jersey 07704
Phone: (732) 933-9800
Fax: (732) 933-4604
Email: bnrl187a@prodigy.com
WWW: www.marketinq.com
Contact: Ms. Marcia Waite
Description: See and analyze all competitor's direct mailings. Database is updated daily and delivered to the marketer's desktop via the internet.
Products/Services: Direct IQ.

Onesource Information Services
150 Cambridge Park Drive
Cambridge, Massachusetts 02140
Phone: (617) 441-7023 (617) 441-7000
Fax: (617) 441-7058
Email: marie_warner@onesource.com
WWW: onesource.com
Contact: Ms. Marie Warner
Description: Business Browser is an integrated on-line information resource that delivers instant access to facts and financial data on thousands of public and private companies and hundreds of industries. It includes financial, news, research reports, executive biographies, and more. Financial data is spreadsheet ready.
Products/Services: Business Browser.

The Roper Center for Public Opinion Research
University of Connecticut
341 Mansfield Rd., U-164
Storrs, Connecticut 06269-1164
Phone: (860) 486-4440
Fax: (860) 486-6308
Email: lois@opinion.isi.uconn.edu
WWW: url:http:RoperCenter.uconn.edu
Contact: Ms. Lois Timms-Ferrara, Associate Director
Description: Largest public opinion database in the World. Free estimates.
Products/Services: Polling Data.

RESEARCH

Teleconnect, Inc.
2701 South Coliseum Boulevard, Suite 1167
Ft. Wayne, Indiana 46803
Phone: (219) 420-1126 (888) 420-1126
Fax: (219) 422-1329
Email: sales@teleconect.com
WWW: www.teleconect.com
Contact: Mr. Martin Screeton
Description: A worldwide provider of business and consumer mailing lists for telemarketing and database marketing operations.

Wilcove Associates, Inc.
14 Medford Road
Morris Plains, New Jersey 07950
Phone: (973) 984-5814
Email: wilinc@worldnet.att.net
Contact: Mr. W. Gregg Wilcove, Ph.D.
Description: Science and technology maps identifying all research driving progress in firms' areas of commercial interest (and all participants' positions in that research), and evaluation measures; for R&D planning, Business Development, License and Acquisitions, and Competitor Intelligence.
Products/Services: Technology Forecasting.

Research Firms

Aaron/Smith Associates, Inc.
34 Peachtree Street NW, Suite 2530
Atlanta, Georgia 30303
Phone: (404) 330-2100
Fax: (404) 330-2110
Email: info@aaronsmith.com
WWW: www.aaronsmith.com
Contact: Mr. Robert Aaron
Description: Consulting for knowledge management competitive intelligence and media analysis.
Products/Services: Competitive Intelligence Knowledge Management. Varies according to project.

Advance Consulting, Inc.
415 North Sullivan, Suite C200
Veradale, Washington 99037
Phone: (509) 880-6024
Fax: (509) 927-5851
Contact: Mr. Charles P. McCoy
Description: Business intelligence support to small and medium sized companies; international and domestic sales and marketing consulting services.
Products/Services: Business Intelligence.

Advanced Information Consultants, Inc.
P.O. Box 87127
Canton, Michigan 48187
Phone: (734) 459-9090
Fax: (734) 459-8990
Email: info@advinfoc.com
Contact: Ms. Laura Schultz

Advanced Technology Advisors
5299 Hickory Drive
Cleveland, Ohio 44124
Phone: (440) 442-1670
Fax: (440) 442-5008
Email: hwata@apk.net
Contact: Mr. Harvey Wiseberg, President
Description: Technical market management consulting.

Applied Marketing Research, Inc.
6750 West 93rd Street, Suite 220
Overland Park, Kansas 66212
Phone: (913) 381-5599
Fax: (913) 381-9444
Email: dphipps@appliedmktresearch.com
Contact: Mr. Donald L. Phipps, Principal
Description: Full-service market research firm providing domestic and international research services.
Products/Services: Market Research

Audience Insight, LLC
2150 Post Road, 4th Floor
Fairfield, Connecticut 06430
Phone: (203) 256-1616
Fax: (203) 256-1311
Email: swolff@ams-online.com
WWW: www.ams-online.com
Contact: Mr. Steven A. Wolff
Description: Market research for cultural organizations.

Baiglobal, Inc.
580 White Plains Road
Tarrytown, New York 10591
Phone: (914) 332-5300
Fax: (914) 631-8300
Email: kpermut@baiglobal.com
WWW: www.baiglobal.com
Contact: Ms. Kate Permut, Vice President of Marketing
Description: Full service market research firm serving clients worldwide since 1969.

Bartels Research Corp.
145 Shaw Avenue, Building C
Clovis, California 93612
Phone: (209) 298-7557
Fax: (209) 298-5226
Email: bartels1@compuserve.com
Contact: Mr. Patrick H. Bartels, Vice President
Description: Research for recruiting focus groups- telephone projects.
Products/Services: Marketing Research Firm

Beyen Corporation
Main P.O. Box 234
Niagara Falls, New York 14302-0234
Phone: (905) 374-4596
Fax: (905) 374-4711
Email: atadini@beyen.com
WWW: www.beyen.com
Contact: Mr. Anthony Tudini
Description: Beyen Corporation specializes in providing retailer pricing and ad tracking services for over 75 product lines in more than 25 countries.
Products/Services: Advertising & Price Tracking Services.

Bourke & Associates
3715 St. Germaine Court
Louisville, Kentucky 40207
Phone: (502) 897-6708
Fax: (502) 897-5398
Email: gregbourke@aol.com
Contact: Mr. Greg Bourke
Description: Competitor and market research. Specializing in managed health care. Publishes Medicare Risk Sales and Disenrollment Report.
Products/Services: Medicare Risk Sales & Pisenrollment Report & Database.

The Burnham Research Group
P.O. Box 118068
Toledo, Ohio 43611
Phone: (419) 726-4283
Fax: (419) 727-8575
Contact: Ms. Aileen M. Smith
Description: Full service research company specializing in customer satisfaction, competitive benchmarking, competitor analysis, market positioning, industry forecasting, strategic planning, monitoring panels, tracking studies and focus group research. Industry specialization: building materials, animal health, health care & medical services, industrial materials & chemicals.
Products/Services: Marketing Research & Management Consulting.

Business Trend Analysts, Inc.
2171 Jericho Turnpike
Commack, New York 11725
Phone: (516) 462-5454
Fax: (516) 462-1842
Email: bta@li.net
WWW: www.businesstrendanalysts.com
Contact: Ms. Kathrine Soscia
Description: Publishes studies covering: food and beverage, chemicals, consumer products, furnishings, equipment.

RESEARCH FIRMS • RESEARCH

CHI Research, Inc.
10 White Horse Pike
Haddon Heights, New Jersey 08035
Phone: (609) 546-0600
Fax: (609) 546-9633
Email: Francis_Narin@compuserve.com
WWW: www.chiresearch.com
Contact: Mr. Francis Narin
Description: CHI Research, Inc. an internationally recognized research consultancy, specializes in developing and analyzing technology and science indicators for use by CHI's corporate and government clients in technology tracking, competitor analysis, licensing negotiations, and related applications.
Products/Services: Technology & Science Consulting Specializing in Patent & Science Indicators.

CMR Consultancy, Ltd.
8, The Causeway
Teddington, Middlesex TW11 OHE
United Kingdom
Phone: 44 181 943 0961
Fax: 44 181 614 8081
Email: info@cmrgroup.com
WWW: www.cmrgroup.com
Contact: Mr. Tony Dent
Description: Specialist supplier of information technology, marketing and market research services.
Products/Services: Market Research

College Marketing Intelligence
140 Prospect Avenue
Arlington, New Jersey 07031-5936
Phone: (201) 998-0173
Fax: (201) 998-4580
Email: 102350.2103@compuserve.com
Contact: Mr. Robert A. Bugai, President
Description: CMI's business intelligence activities are designed to provide timely and accurate market information to decision makers at advertising agencies and packaged goods companies. CMI assists companies in the areas of marketing and promotional services, business intelligence, credit education, and media and program monitoring for marketers of products and services aimed at college and university students.
Products/Services: College Marketing Intelligence.

Competitive Intelligence International
7337 North Lincoln Avenue, Suite 280
Lincolnwood, Illinois 60646
Phone: (800) 963-8080
Fax: (800) 679-9907
Email: cii@compintel.com
WWW: www.compintel.com
Contact: Mr. Steve T. Racz
Description: Competitive research starting with securing public domain, online information to direct, focused, and targeted research on any facet of your competitor's organization.
Products/Services: Competitive Intelligence Benchmarking Research. Hourly billed consulting.

Competitive Intelligence Services, Inc.
2706 South Horseshoe Drive, Suite 110
Naples, Florida 34104
Phone: (800) 278-5004 (941) 594-8003
Fax: (941) 591-0305
Email: jt@compintel.net
WWW: wwww.compintel.net
Contact: Dr. James W. Trullinger, Ph.D.
Description: Research competition, markets, pre-acquisition. Specialization primary contacts, sophisticated analysis.
Products/Services: International Research Firm.

Confidential Security Services
P.O. Box 184
Silver Creek, New York 14136
Phone: (716) 934-0531
Fax: (716) 934-7158
Email: css@james.reg.net
Contact: Mr. William Buchholz
Description: Business Intelligence & Counter-Intelligence, TSCM, Physical & Information & Computer security.
Products/Services: Business Intelligence & Counter-Intelligence.

Contemporary Research
1250 Guy Street, #802
Montreal, Quebec H3H 2T4
Canada
Phone: (514) 932-7511
Fax: (514) 932-3830
Email: luc@crcdata.com
WWW: www.crcdata.com
Contact: Mr. Luc Gauthier, President
Description: Data collection services.
Products/Services: Marketing Research.

Data for Decisions in Marketing, Inc.
2872 West Market Street, Suite D
Akron, Ohio 44333
Phone: (330) 867-0885 (216) 734-4614
Fax: (330) 864-2233
Email: AMERR95071@aol.com
Contact: Ms. Amy E. Merrill
Description: We are located within 30 minutes of Cleveland, Ohio in upscale Fairlawn, Ohio. State of the art focus facility with video taping.
Products/Services: Focus Groups.

Data Security Holding, Inc.
7222 Auburn Lane
New Port Richey, Florida 34654-5805
Phone: (813) 849-0977 (813) 849-4947
Fax: (813) 849-1144
Email: bruschweiler@earthlink.net
Contact: Mr. Wallace S. Bruschweiler
Description: Protection of Corporate Assets and Intellectual Property—Due Diligence—Asset Search on Worldwide Basis—Risk Management—Sensitive Special Assignments.

Decision Making Research
4420 Westover Place NW, Suite 300
Washington, District of Columbia 20016
Phone: (202) 363-8734
Fax: (202) 363-6576
Email: mbmerrin@his.com
Contact: Mr. Mary Beth Merrin, Ph.D., President
Description: ACE—Identifies specific messages that will motivate customers to choose your product/service over competitors. Win/Loss IQ—provides knowledge about why sales were won or lost. Competitive IQ—Intelligence on competitors' activities, and provides early warning signals of new moves by competitors.
Products/Services: Decision Making Research.

Direct Information Access Corporation
P.O. Box 721
Annandale, Virginia 22003
Phone: (703) 978-9428
Fax: (703) 978-5740
Email: diac@cais.com
Contact: Mr. James A. Williams
Description: Due diligence, litigation support, intellectual property protection since 1987.

Dodge Business Research Consulting
3208 West Lake Street, Suite 110
Minneapolis, Minnesota 55416
Phone: (800) 685-7934
Email: dbrc@spacestar.net
WWW: www.spacestar.com/users/dbrc
Contact: Mr. Anthony Dodge, President
Description: 18 years experience conducting qualitative and quantitative market research in the U.S., Europe and Japan. Specialization in business to business and consumer durables.

The Domani Group
8707 Hempstead Ave.
Bethesda, Maryland 20817
Phone: (301) 564-9606
Fax: (301) 564-9606
Email: domani@compuserve.com
Contact: Ms. Christine D. Keen
Description: Anticipate and capitalize on emerging issues important to clients' futures.
Products/Services: Issues Management Consulting/Futures research.

Dupont Investigative Group
1534 16th Street NW, Suite 100
Washington, District of Columbia 20036
Phone: (202) 332-3648
Fax: (202) 332-3672
Email: dig@nicom.com
WWW: www.nicom.com/dig
Contact: Mr. Dana Paul Barooshian
Description: Information about competitors and markets that improves your decision making.

Eureka—Competitive Intelligence
c/o 4112 Landfall Court
Raleigh, North Carolina 27613
Phone: (919) 787-5541
Email: 201-5298@mcimail.com
Contact: Mr. Morton Lurie
Description: Advice on competitive telecommunications products—product line evaluations, functional comparisons, financial analysis of competition.
Products/Services: Network Telecommunications Consulting.

Euromonitor International
122 South Michigan Avenue, Suite 1200
Chicago, Illinois 60603
Phone: (312) 922-1115
Fax: (312) 922-1157
WWW: www.euromonitor.com
Contact: Mr. Eric Restum, Director of Marketing
Description: International consumer market data and analysis.
Products/Services: International Market Analysis.

Explorations
2207 West Addison Street
Chicago, Illinois 60618
Phone: (773) 472-3710
Fax: (773) 529-7401
Email: suegartz@aol.com
Contact: Ms. Sue Gartzman, Principal
Description: Uncover your consumer insight. Focus groups, in-depths, ethnographies.
Products/Services: Qualitative Moderating & Consulting.

Feedback Marketing Services Pvt., Ltd.
1/23, 1-A Ulsoor Road
Bangalore, 560042
India
Phone: 91 80 559 6180
Fax: 91 80 555 0594
Email: feedback@giasbgol.vsnl.net.in
WWW: www.makroindia.com/feedback
Contact: Mr. Ravi Chandar, Managing Director
Description: Business to business studies in India.

Feedback Marketing Services, Inc.
277 Linden Street, Suite 204
Wellesley, Massachusetts 02181
Phone: (781) 235-4449
Fax: (781) 237-5667
Email: fmsinc1@aol.com
Contact: Mr. R. Feige
Description: Intercept surveys.
Products/Services: Research Firm.

The Field House, Inc.
7220 West 98th Terrace
Overland Park, Kansas 66212
Phone: (913) 341-4245
Fax: (913) 341-1462
Email: fhi@rhinc.com
Contact: Ms. Ellen Dimbert
Description: Marketing research company with the ability to complete total project or field work only.
Products/Services: Marketing Research.

Find/SVP, Inc.
625 Avenue of the Americas
New York, New York 10011-2002
Phone: (212) 645-4545
Fax: (212) 645-7681
Email: postmaster@findsvp.com
WWW: www.findsvp.com
Contact: Mr. Andy Garvin, CEO
Description: Experts on call for all your questions.
Products/Services: Quick consulting and research service, annual retainer.

First Market Research
2301 Hancock Drive
Austin, Texas 78756
Phone: (800) 347-7889 (512) 451-4000
Fax: (512) 451-5700
Email: Jheiman@firstmarket.com
WWW: www.firstmarket.com
Contact: Mr. James R. Heiman
Description: Design, conduct, analyze and report marketing research studies—high tech specialty, new product research, product development—North America and Europe.
Products/Services: Full Service Marketing Research Company.

First Principals, Inc.
4440 Warrensville Center Road, Suite 1000
Cleveland, Ohio 44128
Phone: (216) 586-2090
Fax: (216) 586-2309
Email: mfallan@aol.com
WWW: www.firstprincipals.com
Contact: Mr. Michael F. Allan, Vice President Technology Assessment
Description: Technology assessment and commercialization; patent portfolio analysis and licensing.
Products/Services: Technology Transfer & Patent Licensing

Foia Group, Inc.
1090 Vermont Avenue NW, Suite 800
Washington, District of Columbia 20005
Phone: (202) 408-7028
Fax: (202) 347-8419
Email: FOIA@FOIA.COM
WWW: www.foia.com
Contact: Jeff Stachewicz, Esq.
Description: Government information specialists.
Products/Services: FOIA-Ware

D. Frank Research
19425 184th Place NE
Woodinville, Washington 98072
Phone: (425) 788-5633
Fax: (425) 788-0629
Email: dfrank@halcyon.com
WWW: www.dfrank.com
Contact: Mr. Frank Jones
Description: Surveys and focus group discussions for product development and communications.
Products/Services: Marketing Research.

L. Gelfin Associates
8750 Georgia Avenue, Suite 1403B
Silver Spring, Maryland 20910
Phone: (301) 565-9575
Fax: (301) 589-5790
Contact: Ms. Linda E. Gelfin
Description: Specialize in Business Research and Information Strategies. General practice in all industries including healthcare with expertise in Leisure Time Industries.

Greene International
P.O. Box 6636
Portsmouth, New Hampshire 03802
Phone: (603) 433-8883
Fax: (603) 431-6665
Email: greenebenw@aol.com
Contact: Mr. Ben W. Greene
Description: Worldwide business intelligence, risk assessment and security management consulting.
Products/Services: Telecommunications/ information technology.

Griggs-Anderson Research
308 SW First Avenue
Portland, Oregon 97204
Phone: (503) 241-8036
Fax: (503) 241-8716
Email: merris-sumrall@gar.com
WWW: www.gar.com
Contact: Ms. Merris Sumrall
Description: Griggs-Anderson Research is the largest research firm in the Northwest and regularly conducts international research in Western and Eastern Europe, the Pacific Rim, China and South America, in addition to all of its domestic research projects. As a full-service market research firm specializing in technology markets, it has extensive experience in both quantitative and qualitative research. Areas of particular emphasis include product development research, brand awareness and tracking, market positioning, segmentation, choice modeling, market simulation and customer satisfaction.
Products/Services: High technology, market research.

The Helicon Group
P.O. Box 199
Blandon, Pennsylvania 19510-0199
Phone: (610) 916-2081
Fax: (610) 916-2078
Email: helicon@mail.enter.net
Contact: Mr. John J. McGonagle
Description: Provide CI consulting, training and research services. EGA/UTSA compliance.
Products/Services: Competitive Intelligence.

Heskes & Partners
46 Raadhuisstraat
Amsterdam, 1016
Netherlands
Phone: 31 206205859
Fax: 31204200554
Email: heskes@xs4all.nl
WWW: www.xs4all.nl/heskes
Contact: Mr. Sjoerd Heskes
Description: Qualitative market research.
Products/Services: Market Research.

Highsmith & Charnock, Inc.
2912 Sussex Road
Augusta, Georgia 30909-3532
Phone: (706) 733-9548
Fax: (706) 733-9548
Contact: Ms. Doris Highsmith
Description: We have been conducting research in Eastern Georgia, and Western South Carolina for 35 years. Recruit for focus groups, store audits, distribution checks, interviewing, exit polls, mystery shopping, and product pick-up.
Products/Services: Highsmith/Charnock Interviewing Service, Inc.

Information Management Consultants
24534 Framingham Drive
Westlake, Ohio 44145-4902
Phone: (440) 777-2198
Fax: (440) 777-2198
Contact: Ms. Alice Y. Chamis
Description: Planning, design and implementation of competitive information systems and knowledge management systems; evaluations and needs analysis of information systems and centers; information research and management; internet and information training.

Information Plus
14 Lafayette Square, Suite 2000
Buffalo, New York 14203-1920
Phone: (716) 852-2220
Fax: (716) 852-1653
Contact: Ms. Deborah Sawyer
Description: Custom research to assist businesses in decisions about: acquisitions; business development; competitive forces; market entries/exits; and more.
Products/Services: Business Research.

Information Resource Services, Inc.
P.O. Box 200563
Austin, Texas 78720-0563
Phone: (512) 320-8354
Fax: (512) 320-8354
Email: search@librarianoncall.com
WWW: www.librarianoncall.com
Contact: Ms. Renee Daulong
Description: Literature searches, articles reprints, current awareness, corporate library consulting.
Products/Services: Information and Library Services. Business Research.

Infosearch Zurich GMBH
Technoparkstrasse 1
Zurich, CH-8005
Switzerland
Phone: 41 1 445 1885
Fax: 41 1 445 1886
Email: info@infosearch.ch
WWW: www.infosearch.ch
Contact: Mr. Ben J. P. Goette

Infoservice Group
26 Masonbrook Street
Nepean, Ontario K2J 4C5
Canada
Phone: (613) 823-6681
Fax: (613) 823-1175
Contact: Mr. David K. Adams, Managing Principal
Description: Global competition. Changing markets. More demanding customers. It takes a particularly agile, creative and aggressive organization to survive in such a global environment. As business conditions change, so must companies. InfoService Group provides clients with actionable Business Intelligence, and mission-critical competitive insights that permits them to hone in on macro issues and take control their own destinies. Whether we are analyzing foreign markets and competitors, or helping Clients establish their own Business Intelligence System, our work translates into bottom-line gains for our Clients.
Products/Services: Business Intelligence Consulting Service.

Infosmith Research Services
1022 Grape Avenue
Sunnyvale, California 94087
Phone: (888) 611-4636 (408) 736-1107
Fax: (408) 736-1153
WWW: www.imana.com/infosmith/
Contact: Mr. Paul Chan
Description: Research services = patent, trademarks, company, industry, market and competitive intelligence.
Products/Services: Research Services.

Infotree, Inc.
9621 84th Avenue
Edmonton, Alberta T6C 1E7
Canada
Phone: (403) 433-4509 (800) 466-4509
Fax: (403) 433-6537
Email: infotree@telusplanet.net
Contact: Mr. Todd F. Mayson
Description: Patent information specialist, oil & gas industry, chemical, biotechnology and mechanical arts.
Products/Services: Patent Research & Analysis.

Innovative Media Research LLC
456 Ninth Street, Suite 10
Hoboken, New Jersey 07030
Phone: (201) 963-1939
Fax: (201) 795-9685
Email: imresearch@aol.com
WWW: imresearch.com
Contact: Ms. Frane Slater
Description: Check studies and so much more. IMR offers qualitative and quantitative research to meet your marketing needs. Services include: ad testing, from concept to delivers, publication research from development to readership.
Products/Services: Check Studies.

Insights & Directions
1180 East Broadway
Hewlett, New York 11557
Phone: (516) 374-4908
Fax: (516) 374-0398
Email: imcp@worldnet.att.net
Contact: Mr. Howard Willens
Description: Specialize in qualitative research only consumers age 55+.
Products/Services: Gray Matters.

Integrated Software Solutions

815 Industry Drive
Seattle, Washington 98188
Phone: (206) 575-3488
WWW: www.infoharvest.com
Contact: Mr. Philip Murphy
Description: Criterium Decision Plus (COP) is a decision modeling tool for facilitating and presenting recommendations. When making decisions, use COP to organize available information, to bring consensus to group decisions and to justify your recommendations.
Products/Services: Criterium DecisionPlus 2.0.

Intelliquest Information Group, Inc.

1250 Capital of Texas Highway South
Building One, Suite 600
Austin, Texas 78746
Phone: (512) 329-0808
Fax: (512) 329-0888
Email: info@intelliquest.com
WWW: www.intelliquest.com
Contact: Ms. Ursula Talley, Director of Marketing Communications
Description: IntelliQuest Information Group, Inc. is a leading provider of fact-based market information to technology companies. IntelliQuest supplies clients with timely, objective and accurate information about technology markets, customers and products on both a subscription basis and a proprietary project basis. IntelliQuest uses its proprietary databases and software to help technology companies track product performance and customer satisfaction, measure internet/intranet markets, advertising effectiveness, assess brand strength and competitive position, determine price sensitivity and evaluate new products, markets or other business opportunities. The company also designs comprehensive performance measurement systems and provides improvement-oriented consulting services to help clients manage, retain and extend customer relationships. IntelliQuest also licenses proprietary software applications and associated services to technology manufacturers for electronic product registration.

Intercon Research Associates, Ltd.
6865 Lincoln Avenue
Lincolnwood, Illinois 60646-2644
Phone: (847) 982-1100
Fax: (847) 982-1115
Email: global@intercon-research.com
WWW: www.intercon-research.com
Contact: Mr. James D. Donovan, President
Description: Assist companies find valuable new products or enter new markets.
Products/Services: Professional research & search firm.

International Survey Research Corporation
303 East Ohio Street
Chicago, Illinois 60611
Phone: (312) 828-9725
Fax: (312) 828-9742
Email: willw@isrsurveys.com
WWW: www.isrsurveys.com
Contact: Mr. William E. Werhane
Description: ISR is a global firm specializing in the design and implementation of employee, management, and customer satisfaction surveys linked to business performance metrics. ISR's clients include the world's leading government organizations. Over the past 25 years, ISR has conducted surveys for more than 2,100 companies employing over 33 million employees in 106 countries. As a result of our global work, ISR has created globalNorms, which allow for benchmarking of survey results to over 250 norms and benchmarks by country, industry, company performance, and demography. IRS national norms now cover 37 countries.
Products/Services: Employee, management, and customer satisfaction survey.

Inthesis Development Co., Inc.
2840 NW Boca Raton Boulevard, Suite 107
Boca Raton, Florida 33431-6634
Phone: (561) 367-7680 (888) 531-1165
Fax: (561) 362-8011
Email: inthesys@aol.com
Contact: Mr. Sigmund Goodwin
Description: Provide free access to our proprietary database to our market research and statistical analysis clients.
Products/Services: Market Research, Business to Business Assignments.

Ion Incorporated
2111 East Baseline Road, Suite F7
Tempe, Arizona 85283-1505
Phone: (800) 338-3463
Fax: (602) 730-8103
Email: ion@ioninc.com
WWW: ioninc.com
Contact: Mr. Keith Hock
Description: Worldwide referral to investigative sources. Over 19,000 referrals since 1990.
Products/Services: Referral to Private Investigators Worldwide.

Japan Market Resource Network
Yutenji House #1
2-37-22 Nakacho
Meguro-Ku, Tokyo 153
Japan
Phone: 81 3 5721 5990
Fax: 81 3 5721 5993
Email: jmrn@gol.com
Contact: Ms. Deborah Ann Howard

Michael G. Kessler & Associates, Ltd.
237 Park Avenue, 21st Floor
New York, New York 10017
Phone: (212) 286-9100
Fax: (212) 730-2433
Email: mail@investigation.com
WWW: www.investigation.com
Contact: Mr. Michael G. Kessler
Description: Michael G. Kessler & Associates, Ltd., the leader in international corporate investigations, offers a full line of specialty services. With worldwide offices and on staff specialists in competitive intelligence, forensic accounting, and intellectual property protection we can provide solutions to difficult business problems. Services also include Internet monitoring with our Web.Sweepsm and News.Sweepsm programs.
Products/Services: Corporate Investigative Consulting and Forensic Accounting

LBS Associates
104 North Carolina Avenue, SE
Washington, District of Columbia 20003
Phone: (202) 546-2293
Fax: (202) 546-2293
Email: sulc@earthlink.net
Contact: Mr. Lawrence B. Sulc
Description: Corporate intelligence + counterintelligence; counter-terrorism. Law enforcement counterintelligence.

Loan Pricing Corporation
135 West 50th Street
New York, New York 10020
Phone: (212) 489-5455
Fax: (212) 765-4983
Email: dmiller@loanpricing.com
WWW: www.loanpricing.com
Contact: Ms. Dawn Miller
Description: The leading authority on the commercial and industrial loan industry.
Products/Services: Gold Sheets.

Macro International, Inc.
11785 Beltsville Drive
Calverton, Maryland 20705
Phone: (301) 572-0200
Fax: (301) 572-0999
Email: quirk@macroint.com
WWW: www.macroint.com
Contact: Mr. Frank Quirk
Description: Market and survey research and management consulting.

Management Research & Planning Corporation
601 St. Mary's Street
Raleigh, North Carolina 27605
Phone: (800) 347-5608 (919) 856-1144
Fax: (919) 856-0020
Email: mrpci@aol.com
Contact: Mr. John Watkins
Description: MRP is a full service international market and market planning research firm. MRP specializes in market assessments, market planning, competitive intelligence and customer value studies.
Products/Services: Market planning and Market Research.

Maritz Marketing Research, Inc.
1297 North Highway Drive
Fenton, Missouri 63099
Phone: (800) 446-1690 (314) 827-1610
Fax: (314) 827-8605
Email: mmri@maritz.com/mmri
WWW: www.maritz.com
Contact: Mr. Phil Wiseman
Description: A nationwide firm conducting custom and syndicated studies in the U.S. and abroad. Specialists in customer satisfaction measurement. Full-service research in key areas: qualitative, tactical (tracking, AT&U, etc.) and strategic (product positioning, market segmentation, etc.). Fully-staffed local divisions in major market areas; trained, experienced professionals; nation's largest data collecting network. Member CASRO.
Products/Services: Custom Research.

Marketing Intelligence Corporation
P.O. Box 600
Carlisle, Massachusetts 01741-0600
Phone: (978) 369-6628
Fax: (978) 371-0902
Email: murlirao@mktg-intel.com
Contact: Mr. Murlidhar Rao, President
Description: Full service quantitative research & analysis.
Products/Services: Custom.

RESEARCH • RESEARCH FIRMS

Mature Marketing & Research
85 East India Row, Suite 30A
Boston, Massachusetts 02110
Phone: (617) 720-4158
Fax: (617) 723-1254
Email: harrismmr@aol.com
WWW: www.maturemarketing.com
Contact: Dr. Leslie M. Harris, Ph.D.
Description: Dr. Leslie Harris, Managing Partner offers over 30 years of academic, agency, company and field management experience. Terry Pranses provides over 20 years of advertising agency experience primarily in conducting focus groups. Introductory offer: Low cost weekly survey: telephone and/or mail intercept, local, regional or national. Pricing includes tabulation and analysis. One question, three markets, 100 interviews per market-$500.
Products/Services: Omnibus Survey.

McEachin & Associates, Ltd.
P.O. Box 187, Station D
Scarborough, Ontario M1R 5B7
Canada
Phone: (416) 299-4556
Fax: (416) 299-4148
Contact: Mr. Richard McEachin
Description: Specializing in market, company background and litigation support research.
Products/Services: Public Record and Market Research.

Our low cost weekly survey will give you the answers.

Mature Marketing and Research provides an in-depth understanding of the attitudes and needs of consumers 50-plus. Both qualitative and quantitative services.
Areas of specialization include:
financial (banking/investment), travel and leisure, pharmaceuticals, retirement communities and healthcare.

CALL OR FAX:
Dr. Leslie M. Harris, *Managing Partner*
Phone 617-720-4158 Fax 617-723-1254

Mature
Marketing & Research

McGarry Consulting
102 Pembroke Road
Dublin 4,
Republic of Ireland
Phone: 353 1 6685444
Fax: 353 1 6685541
Email: clee@mcgarryconsulting.ie
WWW: www.franchisedirect.com
Contact: Ms. Cheryl Lee
Description: Source strategic business partners for U.S. and European companies.
Products/Services: Business Partnering.

Metromark
3030 Devine St.
Columbia, South Carolina 29205-1844
Phone: (803) 256-8694
Fax: (803) 254-3798
Email: emsmith@sprynet.com
WWW: www.metromark.net
Contact: Mr. Emerson Smith, Sociologist
Description: Target your market and develop products & services that sell.
Products/Services: Business Development

Francesca Moscatelli
506 Ft. Washington Avenue
New York, New York 10033
Phone: (212) 740-2754
Fax: (212) 923-7949
Email: Francesca@bigplanet.com
WWW: dwp.bigplanet.com/qualitative
Contact: Ms. Francesca Moscatelli
Description: Latino Bi-lingual/Bi-cultural focus groups and individual-depth interviews, qualitative research consultant. Active member of Qualitative Research Consultants Association (QRCA).
Products/Services: Qualitative Research Firm.

National Management Services
P.O. Box 861964
Plano, Texas 75086-1964
Phone: (972) 424-8869
Email: natman@dallas.net
WWW: www.dallas.net/homes/natman
Contact: Mr. Larry Bell
Description: Consumer household mailing lists and demographics for metro and suburban Dallas-Ft. Worth, Texas.

PKData
P. K. Data, Inc.
3675 Crestwood Parkway, Suite 280
Duluth, Georgia 30096
Phone: (770) 931-9677
Fax: (770) 931-9564
Contact: Mr. William Kennedy, President
Description: We solve the marketing information and strategic planning needs of middle market businesses. Industry analyses, market assessments, due diligence, competitive intelligence, trade surveys and consumer polling. Decision support for M&A. Computer generated mapping portraying demographics, usage, attitudes and channel management. Industry specializations are healthcare, technology, telecommunications and home and garden.

RESEARCH • RESEARCH FIRMS

Penn Consulting Group
RR1, Box 10 B, Mt. Hunger Road
Hartland, Vermont 05048
Phone: (802) 436-1150
Fax: (802) 436-1151
Email: penncons@aol.com
Contact: Mr. Richard A. Greenlee
Description: Strategic market research and competitive intelligence in the pharmaceutical, healthcare, medical technology, financial and insurance services industries. Customized research, industry and company analyses and profiles, benchmarking and customer satisfaction audits. Call for brochure and to discuss your unique information needs. Strict confidentiality assured. Satisfaction guaranteed 100%.
Products/Services: Strategic Market Research and Competitive Intelligence.

Penton Research Services
1100 Superior Avenue
Cleveland, Ohio 44114-2543
Phone: (800) 736-8660 (216) 696-7000
Fax: (216) 696-8130
Email: research@penton.com
WWW: www.pentonresearch.com
Contact: Mr. Ken Long, Director
Description: Full range of custom primary and secondary marketing research services.
Products/Services: Marketing Research Services.

Perception International, Ltd.
935 Berkshire Road
Grosse Pointe, Michigan 48230
Phone: (313) 822-5012
Email: perintl@aol.com
Contact: Mr. William J. Brazill, Ph.D.
Description: Business Intelligence for corporate CEO's, strategic planners, and institutional investors.
Products/Services: Business Intelligence.

PENN CONSULTING GROUP

STRATEGIC MARKET RESEARCH &
COMPETITIVE INTELLIGENCE

Competitor & Industry Profiles
Benchmarking
Sales Support
Customer Satisfaction

*Customized research in the
Pharmaceutical, Healthcare,
and Financial Services Industries*

RICHARD A. GREENLEE, PRESIDENT
17 Garcia Lane
Hartland, VT. 05048
Phone: 802-436-1150 • Fax: 802-436-1151
Email: PENNCONS@aol.com
website: www.pennconsulting.com

Performance Plus
111 Speen Street, Suite 105
Framingham, Massachusetts 01701
Phone: (508) 872-1287
Fax: (508) 879-7108
Email: PerfPlus@aol.com
Contact: Ms. Shirley Shames, President
Description: Consumer, business, medical market research data collection.
Products/Services: Market Research Firm.

RESEARCH FIRMS • RESEARCH

Pinkerton Consulting Services
Unit A-2, 12th Floor, Union Commercial Building
137 Nanking East Road, Section 2
Taipei,
People's Republic of China
Phone: 886 2 5083126
Fax: 886 2 5080120
Email: mjtsmith@ms2.hrnet.net
WWW: www.pinkertons.com
Contact: Mr. Moray J. Taylor-Smith
Description: Commercial inquires, Litigation support, Business intelligence, Risk assessment.
Products/Services: Commercial Inquiries, Litigation Support.

Porter & Associates
9650 Ventana Way, Suite 202
Alpharetta, Georgia 30096
Phone: (770) 495-7107
Fax: (770) 495-1953
Email: srabauer@porterassociates.com
Contact: Ms. Suzanne Rabauer, Director of Marketing
Description: Market research and consulting firm, specializing in custom research for high technology companies.
Products/Services: Market Research & Consulting

Timothy G. Potter & Associates
1603 Farnam Street, Suite 213
Omaha, Nebraska 68102
Phone: (402) 346-0107
Fax: (402) 342-9379
Contact: Mr. Timothy G. Potter
Products/Services: Competitive Intelligence.

Power Systems Research
1301 Corporate Center Drive
St. Paul, Minnesota 55121
Phone: (612) 454-0144
WWW: www.powersys.com
Contact: Mr. Greg Boeder
Description: Power Systems Research provides international market research, and market strategy consulting for the engine powered products, transportation and power generation industry. Power Systems maintains worldwide production databases.

Prince Market Research
2323 Hillsboro Road
Nashville, Tennessee 37212
Phone: (615) 292-4860
WWW: www.PMResearch.com
Contact: Mr. Dan Prince
Description: National specialists in conducting surveys and focus groups with customers and prospects in order to advise management teams on how to strengthen their companies.
Products/Services: Marketing Research Services.

Projections, Inc.
47 Marlboro Street
P.O. Box 585
Keene, New Hampshire 03431-0585
Phone: (603) 352-9500
Fax: (603) 357-0000
Email: info@PROJECTIONS-INC.com
WWW: PROJECTIONS-INC.com
Contact: Mr. Michael Kenyan, President
Description: Complete domestic and international marketing, research and consulting services.
Products/Services: Marketing Research & Consulting.

Protech India, Ltd.
J-8, Green Park Extension
New Delhi, 110016
India
Phone: 91 11 616 7660
Fax: 91 11 619 6434
Email: chpnotec@giasdlo1.vsnl.net.in
Contact: Mr. Ravindra Singh, Director
Description: India entry strategy, market research, turnkey project management, publishing databases.
Products/Services: Research Firm.

Quality Controlled Services
1375 North Highway Drive
Fenton, Missouri 63099
Phone: (800) 325-3338
Fax: (314) 827-8605
Email: Postmaster@qcs.com
WWW: www.qcs.com
Contact: Mr. Phil Wiseman
Description: QCS is the nation's largest provider of focus group research, combining up-to-date facilities with excellent recruiting. We feature large, modern conference rooms, comfortable viewing areas and lounges, excellent food and amenities, private telephones, quality audio and video taping, and fax services. Our extensive database of consumer, executive, professional, and technical respondents means locating your respondents is faster and more economical. Seven of our facilities are now equipped with FocusVision—a video conferencing service. QCS has developed a national reputation for projects with demanding specifications—quality, consistency, and personal service are all part of our success plan for every group. We offer 35 suites in major markets across the U.S. providing a network of trained professionals to assist you.

Rainmaker Management Consulting
P.O. Box 3092
Pinegowrie, 2123
Johannesburg,
Republic of South Africa
Phone: 2711 787 8208
Email: rmc@cw.co.3a
Contact: Prof. L. Mbigi
Description: African Management, World class management & manufacturing, personal destiny, creativity & innovation, etc.
Products/Services: Rainmaker management consulting.

Ralston Purina Company
Checkerboard Square, 2RS
St. Louis, Missouri 63164
Phone: (314) 982-2056 (314) 982-2807
Contact: Ms. Linda S. Recklein
Description: Provision of electronic and other forms of information retrieval and include document delivery. Types of expertise include trademark, copyright and patent research, competitive intelligence and business/marketing management. Technical areas of proficiency encompass animal and human nutrition, veterinary medicine and food science and technology. Consulting is also provided on the organization/management of information resources from personal to corporate collections.
Products/Services: Information retrieval/consulting. Available upon request.

Real Trends, Inc.
9200 Centerway Road
Gaithersburg, Maryland 20879
Phone: (301) 840-6642
Fax: (301) 840-8502
Email: zhi@tiac.net
Contact: Ms. Zhi Marie Hamby
Description: A nightly electronic newsletter that keeps military, government and business intelligence professionals informed on articles, products and events in the intelligence profession.
Products/Services: ZGram.

Research Online International, Inc.
602 Wellesley
Houston, Texas 77024
Phone: (713) 647-7705
Fax: (713) 647-8076
Email: roi@research-online.com
WWW: www.research-online.com
Contact: Mr. Jonathan H. Leck, President
Description: Competition analysis, strategic planning, market segmentation.

Research Solutions
50 Wingold Avenue
Toronto, Ontario M6B 1P7
Canada
Phone: (416) 781-5106
Fax: (416) 781-8937
Email: jonarnld@idirect.com
WWW: www.capsnap.com
Contact: Mr. Jon Arnold, President
Description: Canada's leading business-to-business market research consultancy. Qualitative, quantitative and organizational effectiveness.

Richardson Consulting Group
2356 Branner Drive
Menlo Park, California 94025
Phone: (415) 854-1598
Email: jlr@rcgc.com
Contact: Mr. John L. Richardson
Description: Technology/Competitive Intelligence—includes technology (product) & commercialization assessments, design & installation of technology intelligence processes; alliance partner and technology source assessments. New Business Development: Market potential, plans.
Products/Services: Technology management consulting.

Rincon & Associates
6060 North Central Expressway, Suite 670
Dallas, Texas 75206
Phone: (214) 750-0102
Fax: (214) 750-1015
Email: info@rinconassoc.com
WWW: rinconassoc.com
Contact: Dr. Edward T. Rincon
Description: Focus groups, survey research, ethnic consumers, demographic reports.
Products/Services: Market Research.

Rodenberg Tillman & Associates B.V.
Spoorstraat 2, P.O. Box 482
Baarn, 3740AL
Netherlands
Phone: 31 35 543 1144
Fax: 31 35 542 5533
Email: rodenberg@rodenberg.nl
WWW: www.rodenberg.nl
Contact: Mr. Joseph Rodenberg
Description: Consultants for strategic marketing and business research. The firm is a network organization, founded in 1985. The firm supports its clients during all phases: business research and intelligence, analysis, strategy development and implementation.
Products/Services: Tillman Intelligence Unit©, Tillman WatchTower©, Business Intelligence Institute©, Perpetual Strategist©.

Roller Marketing Research
290 Virginia Street
Post Office Drawer 1090
Urbanna, Virginia 23175
Phone: (804) 758-3236
Fax: (804) 758-0411
WWW: www.rollerresearch
Contact: Ms. Margaret R. Roller
Description: Specializing in qualitative and quantitative research design, analysis and reporting.
Products/Services: Marketing Research Consultant.

Roper Starch Worldwide
205 East 42nd Street
New York, New York 10017
Phone: (212) 599-0700 (212) 455-4900
Email: info@roper.com
WWW: www.roper.com
Contact: Ms. Carolyn Setlow
Description: Full-service research firm conducting marketing and opinion research in the United States and worldwide. Our mission: to turn data into Intelligence Worldwide. Full custom capabilities include proprietary tools for brand management, customer satisfaction, corporate image management.

Roth Research
4410 South Perlita Road
Tucson, Arizona 85730
Phone: (520) 296-0785
Fax: (520) 296-6545
Email: nroth@azstarnet.com
Contact: Ms. Nancy Roth, Research Director
Description: Intelligence for business development, market growth and marketing efforts.
Products/Services: Secondary research/quote.

Saporito & Associates, Inc.
120 Broadway, Suite 1117
New York, New York 10271
Phone: (212) 227-8575
Fax: (212) 732-4037
WWW: www.brainlink.com/saporito
Contact: Ms. Patricia L. Saporito
Description: Insurance industry marketing and information management consultants. Strategic and tactical focus; qualitative primary research for product/service development and marketing.

Search Corporation
655 Mine Ridge Road
Great Falls, Virginia 22066
Phone: (703) 759-3560
Fax: (703) 759-9778
Email: search1@ix.netcom.com
Contact: Ms. Jean Tibbetts
Description: Technical information, information on technology, research, companies, patents, market research.

Service D'Information Industrielle du Quebec
21 Des Benedictins
Loretteville, Quebec G2A 2V9
Canada
Phone: (418) 843-5384
Fax: (418) 843-8891
Email: legendre@siiq.qc.ca
Contact: Mr. Richard Legendre
Description: Since 1993, SIIQ is a private firm based in Quebec City offering three basic kinds of services: industrial information broker, technology intelligence consultant and business/technology intelligence seminars about implementation within all sizes of organizations.
Products/Services: Technology Intelligence and Information Consultant.

Shafran, Ltd.
3 Nirim Street
Tel Aviv, 67060
Israel
Phone: 972 3 636 1644
Fax: 972 3 636 1643
Email: shafran1@netvision.net.il
Contact: Mr. Michael M. Belkine, Director of Competitive Intelligence
Description: Projects direction and management of local or global scope for all industries.
Products/Services: Business and Competitive Intelligence.

Sierra Market Research
63 Keystone Avenue, Suite 202
Reno, Nevada 89503
Phone: (702) 786-6556
Email: SierraCB@aol.com
Contact: Mr. Carl Bergemann

Solution Engineering
91 Woods Road
East Windsor, New Jersey 08520
Phone: (609) 490-0095
Contact: Mr. Fred Nickols
Description: Solution engineering is a solution-centered approach to business problems. It focuses on linking points of evaluation with points of intervention via structural analyses.
Products/Services: Solution Engineering.

Standard & Poor's DRI
24 Hartwell Avenue
Lexington, Massachusetts 02173
Phone: (617) 860-6512 (617) 863-5100
Fax: (781) 860-6465
WWW: www.dri.mcgraw-hill.com
Contact: Ms. Rebecca Carter
Description: Standard & Poor's DRI provides data, analysis, forecasts and expert advice to more than 2000 businesses, financial and government organizations worldwide. Headquarters in Lexington, MA, DRI/McGraw-Hill maintains offices in New York, San Francisco, Chicago, Atlanta, and Washington D.C. and outside the U.S. in Canada, Belgium, France, Germany, Italy, United Kingdom and Hong Kong.

Stat One Research
2285 Peachtree Road NE, Suite 222
Atlanta, Georgia 30309
Phone: (800) 582-5200
Email: ust@ix.netcom.com
WWW: www.netcom.com/ust
Contact: Mr. Tom Beggs
Description: Provider of industry and custom research to firms of all sizes in publishing, software, telecom, banking, construction, and other industries. Call us and compare our quality, services and rates to that of your current supplier and/or in-house methods.
Products/Services: All-inclusive CPI.

STAX INC.
Stax Research, Inc.
577 Massachusetts Avenue
Cambridge, Massachusetts 02139
Phone: (617) 868-2800
Fax: (617) 868-3381
Email: stax@stax.com
WWW: www.stax.com
Contact: Mr. Rafi Musher
Description: An independent research and analysis group supporting consulting firms, independent consultants, private equity groups and corporations.

Strategic Analysis, Inc.
1125 Berkshire Boulevard, Suite 125
Wyomissing, Pennsylvania 19610-1232
Phone: (610) 320-6100
Fax: (610) 320-6101
Email: StrategicAnalysis@compuserve.com
WWW: www.StrategicAnalysis.com
Contact: Mr. Gregory A. Ramsey
Description: International management consultants: competitor analysis, market research, planning, acquisition assessment.

The Survey Center, Inc.
259 Shore Drive
P.O. Box 400
New Seabury, Massachusetts 02649
Phone: (800) 477-7554
Fax: (508) 477-8877
Email: paulr@thesurveycenter.com
WWW: www.thesurveycenter.com
Contact: Mr. Paul L. Reynolds
Description: Total fulfillment of mail, telephone, and internet surveys.

Systems View
9139 South Roadrunner Street
Highlands Ranch, Colorado 80126
Phone: (303) 683-7454
Fax: (303) 683-0552
Email: dpopken@systemsview.com
WWW: www.systemsview.com
Contact: Mr. Doug Popken
Description: An independent source of quantitative decision making technologies for consultants, corporations and the military. We analyze your situation and develop solutions using techniques like optimization, business process simulation, statistical analysis, risk modeling, forecasting, decision analysis and artificial intelligence. We provide project support, special studies, custom software applications and technical evaluations.
Products/Services: Management Science Consulting.

Technology Market Development Company (TMD)
6 Bach Lane
South Hadley, Massachusetts 01075
Phone: (413) 493-6836
Fax: (413) 585-9322
Email: tmdconsult@aol.com
Contact: Mr. Francis M. Edmonds
Description: Telephone and personal interviewing market research services for management consulting firms that focus on clients serving industrial/business to business markets. Experienced in emerging fast growth technology-based and matured product industries, both small and Fortune 500 companies. Project experience includes research related to new product development, strategic planning, acquisitions and other major investment decisions.
Products/Services: Market Research Interviewing.

Teltech Resource Network Corporation
2850 Metro Drive
Minneapolis, Minnesota 55425
Phone: (612) 851-7500
Fax: (612) 851-7766
Email: rhelgeson@teltech.com
WWW: www.teltech.com
Contact: Mr. Ron Helgeson, Vice President
Description: Teltech is a leading provider of research and content-management consulting services.

Threshold Information, Inc.
1030 Ridgewood Drive
Highland Park, Illinois 60035
Phone: (847) 433-8306
Fax: (847) 433-8932
Email: infopros@threshinfo.com
Contact: Ms. Cynthia J. Lesky
Description: Customized news digests, competitor monitoring. Open source information retrieval and analysis.
Products/Services: Current Awareness/Clipping Services with Analysis. Business Research Services.

RESEARCH FIRMS • RESEARCH

KIRK TYSON INTERNATIONAL

Kirk Tyson International, Ltd.
4343 Commerce Court
Lisle, Illinois 60532-3619
Phone: (630) 969-0100
Fax: (630) 969-3855
Email: ktyson@ktyson.com
WWW: www.ktyson.com
Contact: Mr. Wade Hanson
Description: Kirk Tyson International provides time-based strategic services that drive a company's growth-oriented focus. We apply a mix of competitive analysis, benchmarking studies, M&A support, international business development, and competitive intelligence consulting and training. Accompanied by member firms and affiliates throughout the world, Kirk Tyson International serves most industries.

Urech & Associates, Inc.
12 Norcross Street, Suite 215
Roswell, Georgia 30075-3862
Phone: (770) 552-1030
Contact: Mr. Alan W. Urech

Webminer
2101 Shoreline Drive, Apartment 290
Alameda, California 94501-6205
Phone: (510) 521-4375
Email: mail@webminer.com
WWW: www.webminer.com
Contact: Mr. Jes"s Mena
Description: Data mining services.
Products/Services: WebMiner.

Woelfel Research, Inc.
2222 Gallows Road, #220
Vienna, Virginia 22182
Phone: (703) 560-8400
Fax: (703) 560-0365
Contact: Mr. Adam S. Weinstein

The Youth Research Company
6822 22nd Avenue North, Suite 208
St. Petersburg, Florida 33710
Phone: (813) 384-8182
Contact: Ms. Karen M. Forcade
Products/Services: Child/Teen Research.

Zero Foundation
10-12 Dunlop Lane, Bergviliet
Cape Town, 7945
Republic of South Africa
Phone: 27 21 72 3024
Fax: 27 21 72 6897
Email: weaver@zerofoundation.com
WWW: www.zerofoundation.com
Contact: Mr. Benedict N. Weaver, M.A.(Oxon)
Description: Accurate and timely business intelligence about private companies and individuals.
Products/Services: Corporate Intelligence.

Competitive Intelligence

Burton Knowledge Services
4136 Howlett Hill Road
Syracuse, New York 13215
Phone: (315) 488-0800
Fax: (315) 488-0800
WWW: www.dreamscape.com\burton\bks.htm
Contact: Ms. Cara Burton
Description: Competitive intelligence, knowledge management, corporate library consulting, industry and market research.
Products/Services: Virtual Library Services.

Sharp Information Research
618 6th Street
Hermosa Beach, California 90254
Phone: (310) 379-5179
Fax: (310) 379-1030
Email: ssharp@sharpinfo.com
WWW: www.sharpinfo.com
Contact: Ms. Seena Sharp
Description: Business information and market/competitive intelligence experts. Probes companies, industries, products, services and trends - for new market entry, line expansion, business development, strategic planning. Known for identifying opportunities, threats, substitute competitors, market shifts, emerging niches. Specializes in uncovering future-focused, in-depth, difficult information. Provides analysis and reports. International speaker.
Products/Services: Business Intelligence.

---

strategic market intelligence

- Entering new market
- Expanding product line
- Developing new business
- Identifying trends
- Strategic planning

SHARP
INFORMATION RESEARCH

Seena Sharp
ssharp@sharpinfo.com
310.379.5179 • Fax 310.379.1030

Established 1979

RECRUITING

Business School Career Centers

The Amos Tuck School
Dartmouth College
100 Tuck Hall
Hanover, New Hampshire 03755
Phone: (603) 646-2461
Fax: (603) 646-1295
Email: stevend.lubrano@dartmouth.edu
WWW: www.dartmouth.edu\tuck
Contact: Mr. Steven Lubrano

John E. Anderson Graduate School of Management
Univeristy of California, Los Angeles
110 Westwood Plaza, C201
Box 951481
Los Angeles, California 90095-1481
Phone: (310) 825-3325
Fax: (310) 206-8087
WWW: www.anderson.ucla.edu
Contact: Ms. Kathryn Van Ness

STRATEGIC REVOLUTION: TRANSFORMING INDUSTRIES AND ORGANIZATIONS

AN EXECUTIVE PROGRAM ON STRATEGIES FOR VALUE CREATION AND GROWTH
OCTOBER 17–22, 1999

After a decade of downsizing to enhance productivity and efficiency, world-class companies are using revolutionary strategies to generate growth and profitability.

Learn how to help an organization transition from traditional strategic planning processes to innovative strategic thinking. Assist companies in leading industry change and transforming their internal organizations.

For more information, contact:
Office of Executive Education
The Tuck School, Dartmouth College
Hanover, NH 03755-9050 USA
Phone: 603.646.2839 Fax: 603.646.1773
Email: tuck.exec.ed@dartmouth.edu
Website: www.tuck.dartmouth.edu

Program Faculty Director, Professor Vijay Govindarajan, an internationally known consultant and lecturer, has been cited by *Business Week* as one of the **Top Ten Business School Professors in Corporate Executive Education.**

TUCK AT DARTMOUTH

Chicago Graduate School of Business
1101 East 58th Street
Chicago, Illinois 60637
Phone: (773) 702-1198
Fax: (773) 702-4155
Email: jhuizinga@gsb.uchicago.edu
WWW: GSB.www.uchicago.edu
Contact: Mr. John Huizinga

Columbia Business School
Columbia University, Uris Hall
3022 Broadway, Room 206
New York, New York 10027
Phone: (212) 854-5471
Fax: (212) 222-0390
Email: jpostin@claven.gsb.columbia.edu
WWW: www.columbia.edu\cu\business
Contact: Ms. Judith Kostin

Darden Graduate School of Business Administration
P.O. Box 6550
Charlottesville, Virginia 22906-6550
Phone: (804) 924-7283
Fax: (804) 924-7363
Email: harris@gbus.virginia.edu
WWW: www.darden.edu
Contact: Ms. Ann Harris

Fisher School of Business
Ohio State University
Ohio
Phone: (614) 292-6446
Contact: Mr. Jeff Rice

The Fuqua School of Business
Duke University
Box 90112
Durham, North Carolina 27708-0112
Phone: (919) 660-7810
Fax: (919) 681-6243
Email: drn2@mail.duke.edu
WWW: www.fuqua.duke.edu
Contact: Mr. Dan Nagy

The Georgetown University School of Business
G-1 Old North Building
Washington, District of Columbia 20057
Phone: (202) 687-3741
Fax: (202) 687-8719
Email: wilburj@gunet.georgetown.edu
Contact: Ms. Jacqueline Wilbur, Director

The Goizueta Business School of Emory University
1300 Clifton Road, Suite 320
Atlanta, Georgia 30322-2712
Phone: (404) 727-6399
Fax: (404) 727-8113
Email: samantha_renfro@Bus.emory.edu
Contact: Ms. Samantha Renfro

Graduate School of Industrial Administration
Carnegie Mellon University.
Tech & Frew Street
Pittsburgh, Pennsylvania 15213
Phone: (412) 268-2278
Fax: (412) 268-7094
Email: swaney@andrew.cmu.edu
Contact: Ms. Christine Swaney

Harvard University
Wilder House
Graduate School of Business Administration
Soldiers Field
Boston, Massachusetts 02163
Phone: (617) 495-6232
Fax: (617) 495-8947
Email: kmoss@HBS.edu
Contact: Ms. Kirsten Moss

Indiana University At Bloomington
Graduate School of Business
1309 East 10th Street, Suite P100
Bloomington, Indiana 47405-1701
Phone: (812) 855-5317
Fax: (812) 855-2455
Email: Powellc@indiana.edu
WWW: www.Bus.Indiana.edu/bpoweb/home.html

Johnson Graduate School of Management
Cornell University
217 Malott Hall
Ithaca, New York 14853
Phone: (607) 255-4888
Fax: (607) 254-4522
Email: SFJ1@cornell.edu
WWW: www.intranet.gsm.cornell.edu/cso
Contact: Mr. Stephan F. Johnson

Kenan-Flagler Business School
Campus Box 3490
Carroll Hall
Chapel Hill, North Carolina 27599
Phone: (919) 962-2360
Contact: Ms. Aleta Howell

Krannert GRaduate School of Business
Purdue University
1310 Krannert Building, Room 160
West Lafayette, Indiana 47907
Phone: (765) 494-4377
Fax: (765) 494-6385
Email: Ferrell@mgmt.purdue.edu
WWW: www.mgmt.purdue.edu/mpo/
Contact: Mr. Alan Ferrell

J. L. Kellogg School of Management
Northwestern University
2001 Sheridan Road
Evanston, Illinois 60208
Phone: (847) 491-3300
Email: D-Jacobs@nwu.edu
WWW: www.kellogg.nwu.edu
Contact: Mr. Donald P. Jacobs

Leonard N. Stern School of Business
Management Education Center
44 West Fourth Street, Suite 10-66
New York, New York 10012
Phone: (212) 998-0623
Fax: (219) 995-4224
Email: mohara@stern.nyu.edu
WWW: www.stern.nyu.edu
Contact: Ms. Margaret O'Hara

Michigan School of Business Administration
701 Tappan Street
515 East Jefferson
Ann Arbor, Michigan 48109
Phone: (734) 764-1373
Fax: (734) 763-1250
Email: jwilt@umich.edu
WWW: www.bus.umich.edu
Contact: Ms. Jeanne Wilt

Sloan School of Management
Massachusetts Institute of Technology
70 Memorial Drive, E51-203
Cambridge, Massachusetts 02142
Phone: (617) 253-6149
Fax: (617) 253-0226
Email: ievans@mit.edu
WWW: www.web.mit.edu/sloan
Contact: Ms. Ilse Evans

Stanford Graduate School of Business
Career Management Center
Stanford University
Stanford, California 94305-5015
Phone: (650) 723-2151
Fax: (650) 725-5528
WWW: www.gsb.stanford.edu
Contact: Ms. Fran Noble

THE GLOBAL LEADER IN EXECUTIVE EDUCATION

IT TAKES A PROVEN LEADER TO MAKE ONE

With more than 60 years of experience in executive education, the University of Michigan Business School is a proven leader in developing top-achieving executives. Surveys conducted by international business publications rank Michigan among the world's best in executive education.

Today, successful leadership demands innovative thinking with a global perspective. Executives from all over the world look to our executive development programs to acquire the concepts and high-impact ideas they need to excel in today's competitive environment. These are the leaders who will take their companies to the forefront of the 21st century.

Join the successful business leaders who have benefited from the experience, associations, and expertise only available at Michigan. For more information or a free program catalog call **734.763.1000**.

UNIVERSITY OF MICHIGAN BUSINESS SCHOOL
EXECUTIVE EDUCATION CENTER

Ann Arbor, MI 48109-1234 USA • Phone: 734.763.1000 • Fax: 734.764.4267
World Wide Web: http://www.bus.umich.edu • E-mail: um.exec.ed@umich.edu

Texas Graduate School of Business
2100 Speedway CBA 2.202
Austin, Texas 78712
Phone: (512) 471-7748
Fax: (512) 471-5309
Email: hensonc@mail.utexas.edu/
WWW: www.cso.bus.utexas.edu/
Contact: Ms. Cindy Henson

University of California At Berkeley (HAAS)
545 Student Service Building, #1900
Haas School of Business, Chetkovich Career Center
Berkeley, California 94720-1900
Phone: (510) 642-8124
Fax: (510) 642-9387
Email: dterry@haas.berkeley.edu
WWW: www.haas.berkeley.edu/careercenter
Contact: Ms. Diane Terry

University of Maryland at College Park
Maryland
Phone: (716) 275-4881
Contact: Mr. Robert Hradsky

University of Rochester
Schlegel Hall, Room 203
Rochester, New York 14627
Phone: (716) 275-4881
Fax: (716) 473-9604
Email: junkans@ssb.rochester.edu
WWW: www.ssb.rochester.edu
Contact: Mr. Lee Junkans

The Wharton School
3718 Locus Walk, Suite 50
Steinburg Hall-Dietrick Hall
Philadelphia, Pennsylvania 19104
Phone: (215) 898-4383
Fax: (215) 898-4449
Email: maul@wharton.upenn/edu
WWW: www.cdd.wharton.upenn.edu
Contact: Ms. Ursula Maul

Yale University School of Management
Career Development Office
135 Prospect Street
New Haven, Connecticut 06511
Phone: (203) 432-5900
Fax: (203) 432-6941
Email: mark.case@yale.edu
WWW: www.mayet.som.yale.edu/cdl
Contact: Mr. Mark Case

Executive Recruiters

Acsys Resources, Inc.
1300 Market Street, Suite 501
Wilmington, Delaware 19801
Phone: (302) 658-6181
Fax: (302) 658-6244
Email: dom@acsysresources.com
WWW: www.acsysresources.com
Contact: Mr. Domenic L. Vacca
Description: Permanent and temporary contract staffing for accounting, finance, financial services, and data processing.
Products/Services: Professional perm/temp staffing.

Alexander Associates
993 Lenox Drive, Suite 200
Lawrenceville, New Jersey 08648
Phone: (609) 844-7580
Fax: (609) 844-7582
Email: search@alexassociates.com
WWW: www.alexassociates.com
Contact: Mr. Richard J. Alexander
Description: Alexander Associates is a retainer-based executive search firm servicing Philadelphia, NJ, & NY metro clients.

Ashway, Ltd.
295 Madison Ave.
New York, New York 10017
Phone: (212) 679-3300
Fax: (212) 447-0583
Contact: Mr. Arthur Harelick, President
Description: Specialized since 1977 in science and engineering.

Assessment, Inc.
2600 Van Buren, Suite 2631
Norman, Oklahoma 73072
Phone: (405) 573-9727 (405) 573-9728
Fax: (405) 573-9727
Email: vgettys@ou.edu
Contact: Ms. Vesta S. Gettys
Description: Test development and validation. Expert witness services in hiring, personnel actions. Testing packages for executive selection/promotion.
Products/Services: Psychological Screening/Executive Selection.

Let us introduce you to a wide variety of exceptional growth opportunities currently available at...

Boutique and Niche Consulting Firms

◆

Industry-Focused Consulting Firms

◆

Market-Leading Consulting Practices

◆

Top-Tier and Global Consulting Firms

◆

Emerging Market Consulting Practices

CONSULTING RESOURCE GROUP, inc.
Recruiting Exclusively for the Management Consulting Industry

www.crg-inc.com
ConsultingCareers@crg-inc.com
Phone: (404) 240-5550
Fax: (404) 240-5552

Timing is Everything

Call today for a confidential discussion regarding your career needs and interests.

RECRUITING

R. Gaines Baty Associates, Inc.
12750 Merit Drive, Suite 990
Dallas, Texas 75251
Phone: (972) 386-7900 ext. 224
Fax: (972) 387-2224
Email: gbaty@RGBA.com
WWW: www.rgba.com
Contact: Mr. R. Gaines Baty
Description: Full scale national executive search for specialized mid-to-upper level management in technology systems and consulting firms. Personal attention, results orientation and long term approach. (Twenty years in business of "Targeted" search. Specialize in consulting, technology and general management across most industries nationwide. Career paths in, to and from consulting.)

BG & Associates
10112 Langhorne Court, Suite B
Bethesda, Maryland 20817
Phone: (301) 365-4046
Fax: (301) 365-0435
Email: bgajob@erols.com
Contact: Mr. Brian A. Gray
Description: Recruitment and placement of consultants on a national basis primarily in the areas of information technology, finance/accounting, and human resources.

"Of all the decisions an executive makes, none are as important as the decisions about people because they determine the performance capacity of the organization."
— **Peter Drucker**

R. GAINES BATY ASSOCIATES, INC.
Since 1977
Consulting and Technology Management Executive Search
Dallas & Atlanta

For twenty years RGBA has identified, recruited and delivered the right people at the right time for critical Consulting, IT and General Management positions.
Please contact Gaines Baty at 972-386-7900, x 904 or gbaty@rgba.com.

R. Gaines Baty Associates, Inc.
Global Executive Search Services
12750 Merit Drive, #990
Dallas, Texas 75251
Tel. 972-386-7900, Fax 972-387-2224
Please visit our website at **www.rgba.com**

Howard Bowen Consulting

283N North Lake Boulevard, Suite 111
Altamonte Lakeside Executive Suites
Altamonte Springs, Florida 32701
Phone: (407) 830-8854
Fax: (407) 298-0784
Contact: Mr. Howard Bowen, President
Description: Nationwide recruiting for executives to mid-level managers. Concentration business/manufacturing area. Focus on strategic/implementation experience with SCM, RPD, BPR, other agile/customer issues covering operations and ERP systems applications.
Products/Services: Executive Recruiting

Brindisi Search

10751 Falls Road, Suite 250
Greenspring Station
Lutherville, Maryland 21093
Phone: (410) 339-7673
Fax: (410) 823-0146
WWW: www.brindisisearch.com
Contact: Mr. Tom Brindisi
Description: Work with major and mid-sized national consulting as well as Fortune 500 corporations to identify and place top strategic and change management (BPR) consultants, HR, compensation, benefits, and performance management consultants.

HOWARD BOWEN CONSULTING

Main Concentration on Business/Manufacturing Areas.

Key focus on strategic/implementations capabilities
Provides professionals experienced with solving agile/customer-oriented issues

You too can rely on our expertise as some of the largest management consulting firms have

Processes and Technologies includes:
- Supply Chain Management
- Rapid Product Development
- Business Processes Re-engineering and related support functions, together with ERP Systems Applications
- Implementations with SAP, Oracle, Baan, PeopleSoft.

*Dedicated to delivering Added-Value effectively to
Management Consulting clients at Senior to Mid-management levels*

Member Society of Concurrent Engineering (SOCE)

Altamonte Lakeside Executive Suites, 283 N. North Lake Blvd., Suite 111, Altamonte Springs, FL 32701
Phone: (407) 830-8854 • Fax: (407) 298-0784

Carter McKenzie, Inc.
300 Executive Drive, Suite 250
West Orange, New Jersey 07052
Phone: (973) 736-7100
Fax: (973) 736-9416
Email: carter@carter_mckenzie.com
WWW: www.media-ware.com/carter/
Contact: Mr. Richard Kilcoyne
Description: Information technology recruiting and interim placement.

Consultant Recruiters
6842 North Park Manor Drive
Milwaukee, Wisconsin 53224
Phone: (414) 358-3036
Fax: (414) 358-2660
Email: dwcornell@ibm.net
Contact: Mr. Don Cornell, Principal
Description: Specialist in the management consulting industry for over 15 years. Formerly a manager with two Big-6 firms, with strong IT background.

Consultant Recruiters

Exclusively Recruiting for Management Consulting Firms

Our mission is clearly and narrowly defined: identify and motivate successful consultants to accept new challenges. We work on a retained basis to find managers, partners, directors, and vice presidents for some of the best firms in the consulting industry.

After 10 years as an information technology consultant with three of the Big Six firms, we started this firm in 1983 to help fill the constant need for new talent. We developed a reputation for:

- listening to our clients to learn what they really want and need
- understanding the consulting industry
- connecting with candidates' needs and aspirations
- creatively resolving client/candidate differences.

Today, we have matured to become even better recruiters, using technology to improve our research and focusing on executive level needs. We fill positions that are both most attractive and most difficult to fill.

Don Cornell, 414-358-3036
DWCornell@ibm.net

Consultant Recruiters
6842 N. Park Manor Dr., Milwaukee, WI 53224

Consulting Resource Group, Inc.
100 Galleria Parkway, Suite 400
Atlanta, Georgia 30339
Phone: (404) 240-5550 (404) 240-5553
Fax: (404) 240-5552
Email: mailbox@crg-inc.com
WWW: www.crg-inc.com
Contact: Mr. P. Andrew Robinson
Description: Consulting Resource Group, Inc. is a national executive search firm specializing exclusively in the recruitment and placement of experienced management consulting professionals with top-tier national and boutique management consulting firms.

David P. Cordell Associates
82 Wall Street, Suite 1105
New York, New York 10005
Phone: (212) 285-0634
Fax: (518) 383-4883
Contact: Mr. David P. Cordell
Description: Specializing in recruiting economists for management and executive positions in worldwide financial and management consultant industries.

Cornell Group International, Consulting
68 North Plank Road, Suite 202
Newburgh, New York 12550
Phone: (914) 565-8905
Fax: (914) 565-5688
Email: cornellgroup@juno.com
WWW: www.worldemployment.com
Contact: Mr. Alan Guarino
Description: Prestigious search client base; technology, financial services and healthcare; additionally pioneered internet recruiting beginning in 1994. We service our clients' needs by functioning as consultants and project managers; we do not see ourselves as just an outside vendor. We partner with our clients, move in a common direction and operate with the client's best interests in mind. Offices in New York City, Connecticut and upstate New York.
Products/Services: Executive Search & Contract Research & HR Consulting.

De Funiak & Edwards
1602 Hidden Hills Trail
Long Beach, Indiana 46360
Phone: (219) 878-9790
Fax: (219) 874-5347
Email: BDefuniak@aol.com
Contact: Mr. Bill de Funiak
Description: Recruit insurance and healthcare consultants/managers.

Dieckmann & Associates, Ltd.
180 North Stetson Avenue, Suite 5555
Two Prudential Plaza
Chicago, Illinois 60601
Phone: (312) 819-5900
Email: dieckxsearch@ameritech.net
Contact: Mr. Rick Jeffers
Description: Ranked among top 5 U.S. executive search firms (Sibbald, 1995) in locating and recruiting Partner-level executives for leading consulting and accounting firms.

Dinte Resources, Inc.
8300 Greensboro Drive, Suite 880
McLean, Virginia 22102
Phone: (703) 448-3300
Fax: (703) 448-0215
Email: dri@dinte.com
WWW: www.dinte.com
Contact: Ms. Leah Rogers
Description: Generalist Senior management search firm which exceeds industry standards. Innovative practice in Interim Executives assists clients in accessing finite term expertise for special projects.
Products/Services: Retained Executive Search & Interim Executives.

Drinkwater Executive Search
1 Beach Street
Beverly Farms, Massachusetts 01915
Phone: (978) 922-3676
Email: wdrinkwater@msn.com
Contact: Ms. Wendy A. Drinkwater
Description: Focus on management consulting, IT consulting, name generation, candidate development.

Drummond Associates, Inc.
50 Broadway, Suite 1201
New York, New York 10004
Phone: (212) 248-1120
Fax: (212) 248-1171
Contact: Mr. Chet Fienberg
Description: As a long-term executive recruiting firm for major financial institutions in the tri-state area. We are also in contact with a number of leading consulting firms (primarily New York City based) who are seeking individuals with 5-10 years experience in finance (Banking, Investment Banking, Insurance, Consulting, etc.) in specific areas that include Capital Markets, Risk Management, Information Technology, Operations, and related. Our consulting clients seek aggressive individuals who are willing to travel extensively and who can succeed in that environment. Most situations that come to our attention have partnership potential as long term objective.

Ethos Consulting, Inc.
100 Drake's Landing Road, Suite 100
Greenbrae, California 94904
Phone: (415) 925-0211
Fax: (415) 925-0688
Email: resumes@ethosconsulting.com
WWW: www.ethosconsulting.com
Contact: Ms. Julie Prusak, Vice President
Description: Senior level retainer-based executive search services.
Products/Services: Executive Search

Exec Tech, Inc.
101 West Brighton Place
Mt. Prospect, Illinois 60056-1003
Phone: (847) 797-1880
Fax: (847) 797-1989
Email: exectk@aol.com
WWW: www.bharris.com
Contact: Ms. Bea Harris
Description: Twenty-five years in global contingency and retained search. Interim and start-up executives. Medical devices, biotechnology.

Executive Partners, Inc.
49 Welles Street, Suite 202
Glastonbury, Connecticut 06033
Phone: (860) 657-1458
Fax: (860) 657-1459
Email: execpart@execpartners.com
WWW: www.execpartners.com
Contact: Ms. Holly Seymour
Description: The firm has a reputation for excellence and offers innovative recruiting solutions geared to the management consulting industry. Serving firms worldwide Executive Partners guarantees expedient delivery of leading candidates for practices in technology, reengineering, strategy and operations.
Products/Services: Executive Recruiting

Executive Search Plus, Inc.
401 East Colfax Avenue, Suite 207A
South Bend, Indiana 46617
Phone: (219) 232-1818
Fax: (219) 288-3838
Contact: Mr. Don Walker, President
Description: Search, outplacement and consulting in engineering, MIS and manufacturing.
Products/Services: Executive Search

EXECUTIVE PARTNERS, INC.

Executive Partners, Inc., known for its strong performance, in recruitment for management consulting practices worldwide.

Our web of resources include: a strong worldwide network and extensive database of leading professionals in management consulting. Through captured information about emerging industries, new business management trends, and leading-edge technologies, our searches begin at the doorstep of the right solution.

OUR SPECIFIC FOCUS:
Technology Strategy
Business Process Re-Design
Technology Architecture
Internet Strategy, Marketing and Technology
Operations Management, Logistics, Procurement
Supply Chain Strategies

For more information please contact:
Holly Seymour, Managing Director, Executive Partners, Inc., 49 Welles St., Suite 202, Glastonbury, CT 06033
Tel: 860-657-1458 or visit our web site at: http://www.execpartners.com

Leon A. Farley Associates
468 Jackson Street
San Francisco, California 94111
Phone: (415) 989-0989
Fax: (415) 989-5908
Contact: Mr. Leon A. Farley
Description: Senior level executive search in all industries and functions including outside directors. Scope is national and international through affiliation with Penrhyn International, a global consortium of independent search firms. Retainer only.

James L. Fisk & Associates
1921 Buckington Drive
Chesterfield, Missouri 63017
Phone: (314) 394-5381
Fax: (314) 394-5317
Contact: Mr. James L. Fisk
Description: Specialize in SAP consultants, management consultants, logistics consultants, manufacturing, materials management and healthcare.

The Ford Group, Inc.
485 Devon Park Drive, Suite 110
Wayne, Pennsylvania 19087
Phone: (610) 975-9007
Fax: (610) 975-9008
WWW: www.thefordgroup.com
Contact: Ms. Sandra D. Ford
Description: We are a boutique firm specializing in retained executive search for international management consulting firms and selected general management positions for industry leaders.

Foy, Schneid & Daniel, Inc.
555 Madison Avenue, 12th Floor
New York, New York 10022
Phone: (212) 980-2525
Contact: Ms. Beverly Daniel

Jay Gaines & Company, Inc.
450 Park Avenue
New York, New York 10022
Phone: (212) 308-9222
Fax: (212) 308-5146
Email: jgandco@jaygaines.com
WWW: jgandco@jaygaines.com
Contact: Mr. Jay Gaines

Gilbert Tweed Associates, Inc.
415 Madison Avenue
New York, New York 10017
Phone: (212) 758-3000
Fax: (212) 832-1040
Email: gtany@aol.com
WWW: www.gilberttweed.com
Contact: Ms. Janet Tweed

Halbrecht & Company
10195 Main Street, Suite L
Fairfax, Virginia 22031
Phone: (703) 359-2880
Fax: (703) 359-2933
Email: tomm@halbrecht.com
WWW: www.halbrecht.com
Contact: Mr. Thomas J. Maltby, Partner
Description: We are proud of our reputation for assisting our clients in identifying and selecting superior business professionals dedicated to excellence rather than the merely qualified technician.

Hale Assoc.
1816 North Sedgwick Street
Chicago, Illinois 60614
Phone: (312) 337-3288
Fax: (312) 337-3451
Contact: Ms. Maureen D. Hale, President
Description: Recruiting assistance and research services for executive/managers positions.
Products/Services: Retained.

Harper Hewes, Inc.
1473 Calkins Road
Pittsford, New York 14534
Phone: (716) 321-1700
Fax: (716) 321-1707
Contact: Ms. Deborah Harper
Description: Expertise in recruiting and placing management consultants, with a specialty in information technology consultants.

William E. Hay & Company
Two First National Plaza
20 South Clark Street, Suite 2305
Chicago, Illinois 60603
Phone: (312) 782-6510
Contact: Mr. William E. Hay
Description: Executive selection and organization design consulting to various professional service and consulting firms on a national basis.

Hedlund Corp.
One IBM Plaza, Suite 2618
Chicago, Illinois 60611
Phone: (312) 755-1400
Fax: (312) 755-1405
Email: hedlund@ameritech.net
WWW: www.hedlundcorp.com
Contact: Mr. David Hedlund, President
Description: National management search firm specialized in recruiting information technology and management consultants. Special emphasis on client/server, software package implementers and IT architecture/strategy.

HEDLUND CORPORATION

Executive Search Since 1982

Specialized in placing Strategy, Process and Systems Consultants in all practice areas.

See our website for specifics.

ONE IBM PLAZA
SUITE 2618
CHICAGO 60611
TEL (312) 755-1400
FAX (312) 755-1405
WWW.HEDLUNDCORP.COM
HEDLUND@AMERITECH.NET

Horton Int'l.
217 E. Redwood St.
Baltimore, MD 21202-3316
Phone: (410) 625-3800
Fax: (410) 625-3801
E-mail: mcnamara@horton-intl.com
Web: www.horton-intl.com
Contact: Mr. Timothy C. McNamara
Description: Dedicated global professional services search practice.

Heidrick & Struggles, Inc.
233 South Wacker Drive, Corporate Offices
Suite 4200, Sears Tower
Chicago, Illinois 60606-6303
Phone: (312) 496-1200
Fax: (312) 496-1290
WWW: www.h-s.com
Contact: Ms. Madelaine Pfau
Description: Consultants in executive search assisting client organizations in identifying, attracting and retaining executive talent for specific opportunities within middle and top management and for boards of directors.

Higbee Associates, Inc.
112 Rowayton Avenue
Rowayton, Connecticut 06853
Phone: (203) 853-7600
Fax: (203) 853-2426
Email: rhigbee@netaxis.com
WWW: www.higbeeassociates.com
Contact: Mr. Robert W. Higbee
Description: Specialist to the management consulting industry, strategy operations technology. HAI Technologies, new technology contract division. Specializing in Peoplesoft.

HRD Consultants, Inc.
60 Walnut Avenue
Clark, New Jersey 07066
Phone: (732) 815-7825
Fax: (732) 815-7810
Email: HRD@aol.com
Contact: Ms. Marcia Glatman
Description: HRD Consultants, Inc. is a retainer executive search firm that focuses on human resources. We have successfully completed searches at the Partner level and Associate Partner level, in the Change Management Practices of several of the major consulting firms. For other consulting firms, we have found Compensation consultants.

Human Resources Management Hawaii, Inc.
210 Ward Avenue, Suite 126
Honolulu, Hawaii 96814
Phone: (808) 536-3438
Fax: (808) 536-0352
Contact: Mr. Mike Elinski, President
Description: Our personal careers reflect successful work experience in administration, management, engineering, and MIS. We therefore can better understand your staffing needs and save you time to do what you do best.

The Hyde Group, Inc.
209 Palmer Point, River Road
Cos Cob, Connecticut 06807
Phone: (203) 661-0413
Fax: (203) 622-6314
Email: ahydethg@aol.com
Contact: Ms. Anne Hyde
Description: Nationwide knowledge and network in all facets of management consulting recruiting. Maintain a very strong capability regarding women and minorities in all disciplines.

JDG Associates, Ltd.
1700 Research Boulevard
Rockville, Maryland 20850
Phone: (301) 340-2210
Fax: (301) 762-3117
Email: degioia@jdgsearch.com
Contact: Mr. Joseph DeGioia, President
Description: JDG, founded in 1973 by Joseph DeGioia, formerly with Booz, Allen & Hamilton, Inc., provides executive and technical recruiting covering the functional areas of information technology, supply chain management, business process reengineering, software package implementation, operations research, finance/economics and strategic planning.
Products/Services: Executive Recruiters specializing in Management Consulting.

The Jonathan Stevens Group, Inc.
116 Village Boulevard, Suite 200
Princeton Forrestal Village
Princeton, New Jersey 08540
Phone: (609) 734-7444
Fax: (609) 520-1702
Contact: Mr. Steven G. Goldstein, President
Description: Executive Search—manufacturing, consulting, consumer products, financial services, high technology, marketing, sales, finance, information-technology, publications, category management, specialty consultants, Big 6 experience.

Jones-Parker/Starr
207 South Elliott Road, Suite 155
Chapel Hill, North Carolina 27514
Phone: (919) 542-5977
Fax: (919) 542-1622
Email: jonespark1@aol.com
Contact: Ms. Janet Jones-Parker
Description: Firm specializes in recruiting for the executive search profession including: partner and principal levels as well as identifying firms for mergers and acquisitions.

Richard Kinser & Associates
919 Third Avenue, 10th Floor
New York, New York 10022
Phone: (212) 735-2740
Fax: (212) 735-2741
Contact: Mr. Richard Kinser, President
Description: Generalist executive search firm with specialties in management consulting and communications/marketing communications.

Korn/Ferry International
One International Place, 11th Floor
Boston, Massachusetts 02110
Phone: (617) 345-0200
Fax: (617) 345-0544
Contact: Mr. Mark Smith
Description: Handling full range of industries and functions. Strong international capability through specialty practices, including financial services, consumer products, technology, healthcare, professional services, private equity, education and board services.

RECRUITING • EXECUTIVE RECRUITERS

Kurtz Pro-Search, Inc.
P.O. Box 4263
Warren, New Jersey 07059-0263
Phone: (908) 647-7789
Contact: Mr. Sheldon I. Kurtz
Description: Recruit sales/support expertise-emerging technologies (IT, networking, telecommunications) only.
Products/Services: IT & Networking Technology Consulting

Latham International, Ltd.
8777 East Via de Ventura, #350
Scottsdale, Arizona 85258
Phone: (602) 368-9100
Email: latham@lathamintl.com
WWW: www.lathamintl.com
Contact: Ms. Audrey Lynn, President
Description: Established in 1979, we focus on recruiting "top-tier" MBAs with "fast-track" business experience. Our clients include leading strategy, "Big-Six" and boutique consulting firms nationwide.

LaVallee & Associates
4176 Sulgrave Court
Winston-Salem, North Carolina 27104
Phone: (336) 760-1911
Fax: (336) 760-9511
Email: lavallee@netunlimited.net
Contact: Mr. Michael J. LaVallee, Managing Partner
Description: Recruit information systems consultants. Primary focus on Southeast.
Products/Services: Contingency/Retained Recruiting.

Lawrence Executive Search
32 Reni Road
Manhasset, New York 11030
Phone: (516) 627-5361
Fax: (516) 627-5536
Email: lkamisher@aol.com
Contact: Mr. Lawrence Kamisher, President
Description: Telemarketing, advertising, direct mail.
Products/Services: Assignment - Contingency

Lifter & Assoc.
10918 Lurline Ave.
Chatsworth, California 91311
Phone: (818) 998-0283
Fax: (818) 341-7979
Email: lifters@worldnet.att.net
Contact: Mr. Jay Lifter
Description: Specializing in information technology and management consulting.
Products/Services: Executive Recruiters.

Steve Lombardo & Associates
720 Washington Street, Yale Building
Hanover, Massachusetts 02339
Phone: (617) 826-0317
Email: search@tiac.net
Contact: Mr. Steven Lombardo
Description: Search America provides recruitment services to consulting organizations, retail organizations and product development companies nationwide.

Management Recruiters
3655 Cortez Road West, Suite 90
Brandenton, Florida 34210
Phone: (941) 756-3001
Fax: (941) 756-0027
Email: mriflorida@aol.com
Contact: Mr. Rush Oster, General Manager
Description: Recruiting for general engineering and food, paper, steel, medical industries.
Products/Services: Recruiting Firm

Management Recruiters of Bonita Springs, Inc.
9240 Bonita Beach Road, Suite 3307
Bonita Springs, Florida 34135
Phone: (941) 495-7885
Fax: (941) 495-7686
Email: gfs@bonitasp.mrinet.com
Contact: Mr. Gary F. Shearer
Description: Established in 1992, we recruit nationally for management consulting firms that provide technical, economic and financial services to electric and gas utilities and the pulp paper industry. Our staff provides 50 years experience and qualified mid to senior level candidates that specialize in deregulation, mergers and acquisitions, strategic planning, market analysis, business planning, restructuring, marketing, customer retention, telecom, IT, engineering, and project management.

Martin Stevens Tamaren & Assoc., Inc.
12710 Chateau Forest
San Antonio, Texas 78239
Phone: (800) 465-6114
Fax: (210) 492-4333
Contact: Mr. Bruce Tamaren

MB Inc. Executive Search
505 Fifth Avenue
New York, New York 10017
Phone: (212) 661-4937
Fax: (212) 661-4939
Email: info@mbincexec.com
WWW: www.mbincexec.com
Contact: Mr. Alan M. Levine, President
Description: A national executive staffing resource for marketing, sales and general management discipline, serving corporate and agency clients - consumer and industrial Interim executive services to the marketing, sales and financial communities.

MB Inc.

EXECUTIVE SEARCH & TEMPORARY EXECUTIVE SERVICES

"... A management staffing alternative offering significant organization and cost benefits ..."

At your service to identify, recruit, profile and present qualified executives for positions in:

Corporate Marketing & Sales Management
Communications Agency Management
General and Financial Management

in Consumer Products, Industrial and Financial Service Organizations

Consultants in executive staffing since 1980

505 Fifth Avenue, New York, NY 10017
Tel: 212-661-4937 • Fax: 212-661-4939
E-mail: info@mbincexec.com

The McCormick Group
4024 Plank Road
Fredericksburg, Virginia 22407-4800
Phone: (703) 841-1700
Fax: (540) 786-9355
Contact: Mr. William J. McCormick
Description: The McCormick Group is an executive search consulting firm that is dedicated to providing a comprehensive approach to solving clients' recruiting and human resource needs. We work with our clients on a consultative and interactive basis so that searches are performed quickly and that all important steps in the hiring process are completed in a timely manner. We advise our clients on all significant factors that may effect their hiring decisions. Practice areas include legal, sales and marketing, information technology, real estate, human resources and financial.

Meyer Associates, Inc.
5079 Riverhill Road
Marietta, Georgia 30068
Phone: (770) 565-2020
Fax: (770) 578-1178
Contact: Mr. Rick M. Meyer
Description: Executive search to the management consulting industry, as well as high technology & health care.

Midas Management, Inc.
191 Post Road West
Westport, Connecticut 06880
Phone: (203) 221-2626
Fax: (203) 454-3959
Email: joelb@midasmgt.com
WWW: www.midasmgt.com
Contact: Ms. Elaine Harris, Vice President of Operations
Description: Recruiting for information technology industry; sales representatives through senior management.
Products/Services: Executive Recruiters

Montenido Associates
481 Cold Canyon Road
Calabasas, California 91302-2204
Phone: (818) 222-2744
Fax: (805) 373-5531
Email: swolf@bli-inc.com
WWW: www.bli-inc.com
Contact: Mr. Stephen M. Wolf
Description: Ten years industry experience in re-engineering and information technology consulting prior to sixteen years in executive search.
Products/Services: Executive Search

Nagler, Robins & Poe, Inc.
65 William Street
Wellesley, Massachusetts 02481
Phone: (781) 431-1330
Fax: (781) 431-7861
Email: lnagler@nrpinc.com
WWW: www.nrpinc.com
Contact: Mr. Leon G. Nagler
Description: Serving clients nationally from offices in Boston and Chicago. More than 20-year record of quickly meeting client needs coupled with one of the highest success rates in the search industry.

National Search, Inc.
2816 University Drive
Coral Springs, Florida 33065
Phone: (800) 935-4355
Fax: (954) 755-7913
Email: recruiter@nationalsearch.com
WWW: www.nationalsearch.com
Contact: Mr. Geiger Snelgrove, Operations Manager
Description: Search for the insurance and healthcare industries.
Products/Services: Contingency Search

Don't you wish your competitor's best people would call you for an interview?

We'll arrange it.

The McCormick Group Inc.

The finest name in executive search since 1974.

The finest name in executive search since 1974.

Washington, D.C.
(703) 841-1700
Contact: Brian McCormick

Boston, MA
(781) 239-1233
Contact: Skip Hilton

Paul Winston Norman & Assoc.
5357 West Montrose Avenue, Suite 2
Chicago, Illinois 60641
Phone: (773) 685-4389
Email: pwnco@aol.com
WWW: www.pwnco@aol.com
Contact: Mr. Paul W. Norman, President
Description: Consulting in executive search for executive placement.
Products/Services: Executive Search Consulting

O'Brien & Bell
812 Huron Road, Suite 535
Cleveland, Ohio 44115
Phone: (216) 575-1212
Fax: (216) 575-7502
Contact: Mr. Timothy M. O'Brien
Description: An executive recruiting firm focusing on the recruitment of all functions of senior managers and executives for manufacturing, professional service firms, consumer products and retail organizations.

O'Brien Consulting Services
171 Swanton Street, Unit #72
Winchester, Massachusetts 01890
Phone: (781) 721-4404
Contact: Mr. James J. O'Brien, Jr., President
Description: Retained senior level executive search.
Products/Services: Senior Executive Search

The Onstott Group
60 William Street
Wellesley, Massachusetts 02181
Phone: (781) 235-3050
Contact: Mr. Ben Beaver
Description: Retained Executive Search.

The Partnership Group
7 Becker Farm Road
Roseland, New Jersey 07068
Phone: (973) 535-8566
Fax: (973) 535-6408
Contact: Mr. Peter T. Maher
Description: Human resource consultancy specializing in retained executive search with emphasis on strategic client partnerships. We offer sustained size and critical mass to be effective but are committed to intense personal service.

Paul-Tittle Associates, Inc.
1485 Chain Bridge Road, Suite 304
McLean, Virginia 22101
Phone: (703) 442-0500
Fax: (703) 893-3871
Email: pta@paul-tittle.com
Contact: Mr. David M. Tittle
Description: Executive search and dedicated recruiting services to clients in management consulting, information technology and telecommunications industries.

The Ransford Group
10497 Town & Country Way, Suite 800
Houston, Texas 77024
Phone: (713) 722-7281
Fax: (713) 722-0950
Contact: Mr. Dean McMann

Joanne E. Ratner Search
10 East 39th Street, Suite 514
New York, New York 10016
Phone: (212) 683-1975
Fax: (212) 683-4682
Email: Ratner@ik.netcom.com
Contact: Ms. Joanne E. Ratner, President
Description: Recruiting: management consultants, finance, accounting, marketing.
Products/Services: Finance Recruiting.

Ray & Berndtson
301 Commerce Street, Suite 2300
Ft. Worth, Texas 76102
Phone: (817) 334-0500
WWW: www.prb.com
Contact: Mr. Scott Somers
Description: Executive search and management consulting firm serving major worldwide companies in a variety of industries.

Razzino-Claymore Associates
277 Fairfield Road, Suite 332
Fairfield, New Jersey 07004
Phone: (973) 882-3388
Email: bcasillo@bellatlantic.net
Contact: Ms. Janelle Razzino
Description: A boutique search firm offering the foremost in executive recruiting with a personal touch.

Jack Richman & Associates
P.O. Box 25412
Ft. Lauderdale, Florida 33320
Fax: (954) 389-9572
Email: jrafl@aol.com
WWW: misjobs.com/jra
Contact: Mr. Jack Richman, President
Description: Client server telecommunications, midrange, executive recruiting.

The Rubicon Group
7553 East Santa Catalina Drive
Scottsdale, Arizona 85255
Phone: (602) 515-9225
Fax: (602) 515-9213
Email: Judyjacobs@aol.com
Contact: Mr. Martin Jacobs, Manager
Description: Medical profession- administrative nurses, directors nurses, nurse managers.
Products/Services: Search Consultants.

Sales Consultants of Princeton, Inc.
1230 Parkway Avenue, Suite 102
West Trenton, New Jersey 08628
Phone: (609) 882-8388
Fax: (609) 882-4862
Email: princetn!rjb@mrinet.com
Contact: Mr. Robert J. Bodnar, President
Description: Professional consulting firm specializing in executive search/consulting services.
Products/Services: Executive Search.

Santangelo Consultants, Inc.
60 E. 42nd Street, Suite 1333
New York, New York 10165
Phone: (212) 867-6664
Fax: (212) 370-9071
Contact: Mr. Richard Santangelo
Description: Placement of experienced management consultants in information systems, process management, financial service and healthcare industries. Our clients are prestigious management consulting firms. Emphasis on information systems, operations improvement, productivity, healthcare, banking, brokerage, insurance, finance, management accounting, strategic planning, inventory planning and control systems.

Savoy Partners, Ltd.
1620 L Street NW, Suite 801
Washington, District of Columbia 20036
Phone: (202) 887-0666
Email: savoyon@bellatlantic.net
Contact: Mr. Robert J. Brudno
Description: Senior level, retained executive search firm with 18 years of recruiting professionals for consulting firms.

SCSD, Inc.
111 Prospect Street, Suite 410
Stamford, Connecticut 06901
Phone: (203) 327-3270
Fax: (203) 327-6578
Email: scstamford@aol.com
Contact: Mr. James M. Burt
Description: Specialists in training and sales/marketing professionals for the consulting industry.

Search America, Inc.
678 Burmont Road, Suite 600-K
Drexel Hill, Pennsylvania 19026
Phone: (610) 259-2800
Contact: Mr. Thomas V. Giacoponello
Description: Searches focus on such areas as HR consulting, strategic planning and data base consulting as well as market research positions within a consultancy.

Seco & Zetto Assoc., Inc.
P.O. Box 225
Harrington Park, New Jersey 07640
Phone: (201) 784-0674
Contact: Mr. William M. Seco
Description: Information technology, consulting, sales.

Spear-Izzo Assoc.
651 Holiday Drive, Suite 300
Foster Plaza, Building Five
Pittsburgh, Pennsylvania 15220-2740
Phone: (412) 928-3290
Fax: (412) 561-9091
Email: info@siasearch.com
WWW: www.siasearch.com
Contact: Mr. Kenneth T. Spear, Partner
Description: Specialized, since 1972, in providing executive search for management consulting industry. Serve most types of firms (general business, process/productivity improvement, strategic, engineering, etc.). Permanent, temporary and contract placements - both retained and contingency fee arrangements.
Products/Services: Executive Recruiting/Search specializing in Management Consulting

Spencerstuart
1717 Main Street, Suite 5300
Dallas, Texas 75201-4605
Phone: (214) 658-1777
Contact: Mr. Randall D. Kelley
Description: CEO, senior level executive and board of director search consulting services.

The Stark Wilton Group
P.O. Box 4924
East Lansing, Michigan 48826
Phone: (517) 332-4100
Fax: (517) 332-2377
Email: starkwiltongroup@worldnet.att.net
Contact: Ms. Mary Stark
Description: The Stark Wilton Group specializes in providing personalized services to a select group of clients. We specialize in the functional areas of consulting, sales & marketing and finance.

Strategic Executives, Inc.
6 Landmark Square, 4th Floor
Stamford, Connecticut 06901
Phone: (203) 359-5757
Fax: (203) 978-1785
Email: gulian@stratsearch.com
WWW: www.strategicexecutives.com
Contact: Mr. Randolph Gulian
Description: National search and selection programs designed to identify management consultants, marketing executives and corporate business planning and development professionals for client companies wishing to enhance their competitive position.

Synergistics Assoc., Ltd.
400 North State Street, Suite 400
Chicago, Illinois 60610
Phone: (312) 467-5450
Contact: Mr. Alvin J. Borenstine
Description: 100% retainer executive search firm specializing in information technology, CIO's and senior level consultants.

M. L. Tawney & Associates
P.O. Box 630573
Houston, Texas 77263-0573
Phone: (713) 784-9163
Email: mtawney@ix.netcom.com
Contact: Mr. Mel Tawney
Description: Executive search, mergers and acquisitions on an international basis. Associates in Western Europe, Far East, Central and South America and Australia.

Carl J. Taylor & Co.
11551 Forest Central Drive, Suite 329
Dallas, Texas 75243
Phone: (214) 340-1188
Fax: (214) 340-1175
Contact: Mr. Carl J. Taylor, President
Description: Carl Taylor has over twenty years of experience in the management consulting and executive search professions. He has successfully recruited consulting professionals at all levels and in many functional areas, including information technology, financial analysis, strategy and operations.
Products/Services: Executive Search.

"Our backlog is overflowing"

"Our clients need more services"

"If only we had more of the right professionals..."

Sound Familiar?

In a highly competitive, rapidly growing business environment, your firm needs an executive search consultant who is:

Professional
Personal
Productive

Carl J. Taylor & Co.

11551 Forest Central Drive, Ste. 329, Dallas, TX 75243
Phone: 214-340-1188   Fax: 214-340-1175

> **OUR SEASONED RECRUITERS ARE LOOKING TO EARN YOUR TRUST AND RESPECT**
>
> Servicing the Consulting Industry
> with
> Effective Executive Search.
> Retainer & Contingency
>
> *Areas of specialization:*
> Compensation, Benefits, Actuarial, Healthcare, Health & Welfare, Benefits Administration, Human Resources and Management Consulting
>
> 1N 141 County Farm Rd., Winfield, Il. 60190
> 630-690-0055 • Fax: 630-690-5533

Waterford Executive Group Ltd.
1 N. 141 County Farm Road, Suite 220 D
Winfield, Illinois 60190
Phone: (630) 690-0055
Fax: (630) 690-5533
Email: waterfrd@wwa.com
Contact: Mr. Patrick Atkinson
Description: Committed to servicing the consulting industry with our seasoned staff of professional recruiters.

Watson International, Inc.
25 West 43rd Street, Suite 914
New York, New York 10036
Phone: (212) 354-3344
Fax: (212) 354-3348
Email: hwatson@watsoninternational.com
WWW: www.watsoninternational.com
Contact: Mrs. Hanan S. Watson, President
Description: Executive search with focus on the energy industry.
Products/Services: Retained executive search.

Weinstein & Company
One Apple Hill, Suite 316
Natick, Massachusetts 01760
Phone: (508) 655-3838
Contact: Mr. Lewis R. Weinstein
Description: Former Bain consultant has multi-specialty search practice which includes finding senior people for consulting firms. National practice: consulting firms, media/entertainment/convergence, consumer products, financial services.

Daniel Wier & Assoc.
333 South Grand Avenue, Suite 1880
Los Angeles, California 90071
Phone: (213) 628-2580
Fax: (213) 628-2581
Email: Dancwier@aol.com
Contact: Mr. Daniel C. Wier
Description: Executive search services for national and regional consulting firm with an unsurpassed ratio of success.

Wilson-Douglas-Jordan
70 West Madison, Suite 1400
Chicago, Illinois 60602
Phone: (312) 782-0286
Contact: Mr. John T. Wilson
Description: Retained search specializing in information technology and management consultants.

Bob Wright Recruiting, Inc.
56 DeForest Road
Wilton, Connecticut 06897-1907
Phone: (203) 762-9046
Fax: (203) 762-5807
Contact: Mr. J. Robert Wright, President
Description: Contingency placement of sales and marketing talent in services industries.

SOFTWARE

Software

DeLaura Development Co., L.L.C.
P.O. Box 328
East Lyme, Connecticut 06333
Phone: (860) 691-1524
Fax: (860) 691-1524
Email: busvitalsigns@snet.net
WWW: www.busvitalsigns.com
Contact: Mr. Edward D. J. DeLaura, President
Description: Intuitive financial analysis & management program for MS Windows.
Products/Services: Business Vital Sign System.

Attract New Business Clients

Open New Doors With Quick Diagnostics And Achieve Outstanding Financial Results.

You and your clients will work smarter, take command of financials and manage the vital signs for outstanding results with

Business Vital Signs™ for Windows.

You will:
- *Get up and running on Day One*
- *Quickly see financial trends and problems*
- *Perform fast financial assessments*
- *Track & analyze unlimited businesses*
- *Create financial models and plan improvements*
- *Design affordable growth scenarios*
- *Make better decisions in half the time*
- *Make higher profits for you and your clients*

Free Trial And Money Back Guarantee

See our web site at **http://www.busvitalsigns.com**
or E-mail: **busvitalsigns@snet.net**

DeLaura Development Co., LLC

SOFTWARE • SOFTWARE

Micrografx
1803 East Arapaho Road
Richardson, Texas 75081
Phone: (972) 994-6156
Fax: (972) 994-6227
Email: carlg@micrografx.com
WWW: www.micrografx.com
Contact: Mr. Carl Griffith, Director of Enterprise Sales, N. America
Description: Start with Micrografx FlowCharter®, the most efficient tool for documenting business processes. Then there's Optima™, the easy-to-use graphical process simulation tool that lets you test your ideas, and see results before changes are made. For SAPr professionals, EnterpriseCharter™ is the essential graphical toolkit for visualizing and deploying the R/3™ system. And don't forget ISOCharter™, the fastest route to ISO/QS-9000 registration.
Products/Services: Optima, ISOCharter, FlowCharter, EnterpriseCharter

Moneysoft, Inc.
1 East Camelback Road #550
Phoenix, Arizona 85012
Phone: (800) 966-7797
Email: mbray@moneysoft.com
Contact: Mr. Michael B. Bray
Description: Business requestion software system to analyze, value, prize, structure, and finance deals.
Products/Services: Buy-Out Plan

Open Door Software
2814 East Bearss Avenue
Tampa, Florida 33613
Phone: (800) 837-8636
Fax: (813) 972-7986
Email: opendoor@tervo.com
WWW: www.tervo.com
Contact: Ms. Tina Kattos, Marketing Director
Description: Provider of groupware, database and conversion solutions using Visual Basic, Visual FoxPro, Microsoft Outlook and Exchange Server.
Products/Services: B.I.G.Brother '98.

Palisade Corporation
31 Decker Road
Newfield, New York 14867
Phone: (607) 277-8000
Fax: (607) 277-8001
Email: sales@palisade.com
WWW: www.palisade.com
Contact: Mr. Joseph Prisco, Technical Marketing
Description: Risk and decision analysis software, featuring @RISK and Precision Tree.
Products/Services: Project Management.

Signature Software, Inc.
489 North 8th Street, Suite 201
Hood River, Oregon 97031
Phone: (800) 925-8840 (541) 386-3221
WWW: www.signaturesoftware.com
Contact: Mr. Michael Benedict
Description: Signature Software creates a truetype font from a one page handwriting sample. This allows our customers to type in their own handwriting—even "hand address" envelopes.
Products/Services: Custom Handwriting Fonts.

Accounting

Accountmate Software Corporation
20 Sunny Side Avenue, Suite C
Mill Valley, California 94941
Phone: (415) 381-1011 (800) 877-8896
Fax: (415) 381-6902
Email: info@accountmate.com
WWW: accountmate.com
Contact: Mr. Joel Fallon
Description: The award winning suite of Visual AccountMate accounting modules presents the same user interface on all the most popular platforms and databases. Certified for Windows NT and BackOfffice, these Year 2000 ready products optimize both the Microsoft BackOffice and IBM DB2 databases. AccountMate makes its true 32-bit Visual FoxPro 5.0 source code available to resellers, allowing for customization to meet almost any specific accounting need.
Products/Services: Visual AccountMate.

Checkmark Software, Inc.
724 Whalers Way, Building H
Ft. Collins, Colorado 80525
Phone: (800) 444-9922
Fax: (970) 225-0611
Email: karl@checkmark.com
WWW: www.checkmark.com
Contact: Mr. Karl Kleinbach
Description: MultiLedger combines Accounts Receivable, Accounts Payable, Inventory and General Ledger into one easy-to-use program. Built in multiuser capabilities for up to 10 users. "It is ideal for your small business clients looking for a package somewhere between the entry-level systems and the expensive ones." -Computers in Accounting.
Products/Services: CheckMark payroll, MultiLedger.

Comptrol, Inc.
2543 152nd Avenue NE
Redmond, Washington 98052
Phone: (425) 869-2700
Fax: (425) 869-1157
Email: michelle@comptrol.net
WWW: www.comptrol.net
Contact: Ms. Michelle Meeks, Job Cost Technical Support
Description: Job Cost Software for SBT Pro Series Accounting.

Core Software, Inc.
26303 Oak Ridge Drive
Spring, Texas 77380
Phone: (281) 292-2177
Fax: (281) 298-1492
Email: core@coresoftware.com
WWW: www.coresoftware.com
Contact: Mr. Mark Watthuber
Description: Core Software, Inc. develops FasTrak Service Management Software. This software helps users control all phases of their business, from receipt of a service request to billing the customer, to analyzing profitability. Since 1982, Core Software has successfully automated over 1200 businesses. And, with the new Windows screens, and the powerful Crystal Reports report writer, the modularized FasTrak system is helping both small and large companies fulfill their growing needs.
Products/Services: FasTrak.

Cougar Mountain Software
7180 Potomac Drive, Suite D
Boise, Idaho 83704
Phone: (800) 388-3038 (208) 375-4455
Fax: (208) 375-4460
Email: sales@cougarmtn.com
WWW: www.cougarmtn.com
Contact: Mr. Dave Lakhani
Description: Cougar Mountain Software pioneered the Accounting and Point of Sale software market more than 16 years ago. Today they continue to dominate the mid-range accounting and point of sale market with their integrated Accounting for Windows, ACTPlus, FUND Accounting, FUND Accounting for Windows, as well as Point of Sale for Windows and StoreWare. More than 25,000 businesses rely on Cougar Mountain Software each day to run the vital financial functions of their business. As part of their focused effort to remain leaders in the market, Cougar Mountain recently released the Point of Sale Power Station, an integrated POS hardware and software solution for retailers, the price starts at very moderate $2995.00. POS hardware is also available.
Products/Services: Act Plus Accounting System.

Daceasy, Inc.
17950 Preston Road
Dallas, Texas 75252
Phone: (800) 322-3279 (972) 732-7500
Fax: (972) 713-6331
WWW: www.daceasy.com
Contact: Sales
Description: Full featured, easy to use accounting system for small businesses. DacEasy integrates accounting, invoicing, payroll, communications, and management software into a single package.
Products/Services: DacEasy Accounting and Payroll.

SOFTWARE • ACCOUNTING

Farin & Assoc., Inc.
6506 Schroeder Road
Madison, Wisconsin 53711
Phone: (800) 236-3724
Fax: (608) 273-2374
Email: jbraeger@farin.com
WWW: www.farin.com
Contact: Mr. John Braeger, Marketing Director
Description: Asset/liability consulting, education and software, website development.
Products/Services: SAM/CyFi Financial.

Open Systems, Inc.
7626 Golden Triangle Drive
Eden Prairie, Minnesota 55344
Phone: (612) 829-0011
Fax: (612) 829-1400
WWW: www.osas.com
Contact: Mr. Brian Buckley
Description: Traverse '97, the newest product line from Open Systems, is an integrated accounting solution that incorporates true 32 Bit multi/tasking/threading architecture, with features such as an interface to M/S Office. Other features include inter/intranet access, source code control, multi-page previews and more. Traverse '97 includes AP, AR, GL, SO, PO and Bank Rec.
Products/Services: Traverse '97.

System Technology Group
21053 Devonshire Street, #106
Chatsworth, California 91311
Phone: (818) 718-0990
WWW: systechgrp.com
Contact: Mr. Mel Mitchell
Description: Windows based software for manufacturing distribution, retail and service companies.
Products/Services: Great Plains Software.

Systematic Solutions
2845 Moorpark Avenue, Suite 112
San Jose, California 95128
Phone: (408) 379-1111
Fax: (408) 364-1947
Email: jcozens@systematicsol.com
WWW: www.systematicsol.com
Contact: Mr. Jeff Cozens, President
Description: Accounting software for service, non-profit and distribution industry.
Products/Services: Solomon IV., Touchstone/2000 Software.

Zoom Systems, Inc.
1025 N. Central Expressway, Suite 300-111
Plano, Texas 75025
Phone: (972) 398-7874
Fax: (972) 398-7874
Email: zoom@saxena.com
WWW: www.saxena.com/zoom
Contact: Mr. Avi Saxena, President
Description: C/ctt, Java, VB, SQL server software development.
Products/Services: Software development.

Business Plan Presentation

E-Strategy
10 Av. Jef Lambeaux
Brussels, B-1060
Belgium
Phone: 32 2 534 34 00
Fax: 32 2 537 60 18
Email: lamoffett@compuserve.com
Contact: Mr. Larry A. Moffett
Description: Business management software and consulting: desktop applications for marketing strategy, business plans, sales forecasting, risk analysis, decision analysis, dynamic simulation, conjoint analysis, activity-based costing and more.
Products/Services: MBA-Ware.

Global Travel Apartments
1000 Yonge Street
Toronto, Ontario M4W 2K2
Canada
Phone: (416) 923-1000 (800) 667-8483
Fax: (416) 924-2446
Email: info@globaltrvlapt.com
WWW: www.globaltrvlapt.com
Contact: Mr. Thomas F. Vincent
Description: Canada's leading provider of worldwide temporary furnished accommodations, for the consultants who are on short-term assignment, on a training program or relocating. Covering Toronto and eight other Canadian cities, plus 125 cities in 26 countries worldwide.
Products/Services: Corporate furnished apartments and housing.

Out of Your Mind . . . and Into the Marketplace™
13381 White Sand Drive
Tustin, California 92780
Phone: (714) 544-0248 (714) 544-0248
Fax: (800) 419-1513
WWW: www.business-plan.com/
Contact: Ms. Jackirae Sagouspe, Marketing Director
Description: Stand alone software for IBM & Comparibles. Guides user through complete business planning process including organizational plan, marketing plan, and financial plan with financial statement analysis. All spreadsheets pre-formatted and pre-formulated.
Products/Services: Automate Your Business Plan (6.0 for Windows 3.1 or 95).

Synquest, Inc.
3500 Parkway Lane, Suite 555
Norcross, Georgia 30092
Phone: (770) 447-8667
Fax: (770) 447-4995
Email: info@synquest.com
WWW: www.synquest.com
Contact: Mr. Art Brown
Description: Optimum, integrated strategic development for worldwide supply chain management.
Products/Services: Strategic Supply Chain Consulting.

Contact Management

Maximizer Technologies, Inc.
1090 West Pender Street, 9th Floor
Vancouver, British Columbia V6E 2N7
Canada
Phone: (800) 804-6299 (604) 601-8000
Fax: (604) 601-8077
Email: sales@maximizer.com
WWW: www.maximizer.com/
Contact: Mr. Stephen Brooks
Description: Maximizer is the world's most powerful contact management software. With Maximizer, you pinpoint new prospects, keep up with customers, and turbocharge your sales.
Products/Services: Maximizer.

Sage U.S., Inc.
17950 Preston Road, Suite 800
Dallas, Texas 75252
Phone: (800) 835-6244 (972) 733-4292
Fax: (972) 733-4251
WWW: www.telemagic.com
Contact: Mr. Sales
Description: Contact management solution provides an integrated calendar, contact database, multi-media communications (email, paging, faxing, direct mail) solution for individual or network users using a fully relational database.
Products/Services: TeleMagic for Windows.

West/Marketing Associates
3551 South Monaco Parkway, Suite 281
Denver, Colorado 80237
Phone: (303) 759-9247
WWW: www.westmarketing.com
Contact: Mr. Ed Fuller
Description: Marketing automation software for loyalty marketing and frequent buyer programs.
Products/Services: Loyalty Magic.

Document Management

Axon, Inc.
One Stamford Landing
62 Southfield Avenue
Stamford, Connecticut 06902
Phone: (203) 357-9701
Fax: (203) 324-5085
Email: info@axoninc.com
WWW: www.axoninc.com
Contact: Ms. Susan Rhame
Description: Solo is a high end report production software package for Windows and MacIntosh. Solo contains hundreds of consulting type templates for fast preparation of business reports. Axon provides consulting services for report design and customization of the Template library.
Products/Services: Solo™

Comprose
2249 South Brentwood Boulevard
St. Louis, Missouri 63144
Phone: (800) 348-8211
Fax: (314) 968-5442
Email: comprose@inlink.com
WWW: www.comprose.com
Contact: Ms. Teresa Tarwater
Description: Create, manage and web publish policies and procedures quickly and easily.
Products/Services: ProcedureWRITE.

CREATING CLIENT REPORTS SHOULDN'T TAKE A MIRACLE

SOLO™
VISUAL COMMUNICATION

Do you need divine intervention to create effective, client ready reports?

Solo™ is a high end, software tool to help consulting and professional firms produce professionally designed, convincing reports.

Solo makes the process of creating visually appealing, effective client communications easy and less time consuming.

- Storyboarding - helps make sure your storyline is logical
- Built in consulting graphics, Solo's Template Library - makes choosing the correct graphic to illustrate your message effortless
- Customizable document format - ensures your corporate identity is known, no matter who creates the report, enabling you to concentrate on content not format
- Powerful knowledge management features allow easy sharing of accumulated knowledge

Axon Incorporated

One Stamford Landing, 62 Southfield Avenue, Stamford, CT 06902
Phone: (203) 357-9701   Fax: (203) 324-5085
Web: http://www.axoninc.com   E-mail: info@axoninc.com

Infoimage, Inc.
100 West Clarendon, Suite 2310
Phoenix, Arizona 85013
Phone: (800) 489-9511
Fax: (602) 234-6950
Email: msantos@infoimage.com
WWW: www.infoimage.com
Contact: Ms. Marilena Santos
Description: Offices in AZ, CA, CO, IL, MA, NY, TX, WA.
Products/Services: Interactive Self Service Solutions.

Printovation
P.O. Box 64499
St. Paul, Minnesota 55164-9650
Phone: (800) 386-7127
Fax: (800) 386-7128
Email: printovation@taylor.com
WWW: www.printovation.com
Contact: Mr. Jeff Roll
Description: Printovation is a software that works with Microsoft Word and Publisher. It allows you to order either one, two, or full color printing from the comfort of your home or office.
Products/Services: Short run digital printing.

Intelligence/Expert/Modeling

ABCTechnologies, Inc.
16100 NW Cornell Road, Suite 200
Beaverton, Oregon 97006
Phone: (503) 617-7100 (503) 617-7150
Fax: (503) 617-7200
Email: rickm@abctech.com
WWW: www.abctech.com
Contact: Mr. Rick Musser
Description: Our world leading Activity-Based Information System is for every level of an ABC/M project, starting from a pilot and scaling up to enterprise-wide implementations. Our Client Services department offers: all levels of ABC/M education; technical experts which consultants and clients can leverage for on site services; and our Technical Support which is renown for its accessibility and excellent response time. Through our Affiliate Program, we partner with carefully selected management consultants who leverage our software and services as they provide project management and implementation assistance around a broad set of business improvement initiatives.
Products/Services: Activity-based Costing Software.

Blue Marble Development Group, Inc.
406 Amapola Avenue, Suite 125
Torrance, California 90501
Phone: (310) 328-3583
Fax: (310) 328-9057
Email: drmmmann@pacbell.net
Contact: Dr. Michael M. Mann, CMC, President
Description: Organizational & business process analysis and design; knowledge management.
Products/Services: EnCompassr

Business Forecast Systems, Inc.
68 Leonard Street
Belmont, Massachusetts 02478
Phone: (617) 484-5050
Fax: (617) 484-9219
Email: info@forecastpro.com
WWW: www.forecastpro.com
Contact: Mr. Eric Stellwagen, Vice President
Description: Accurate affordable forecasting solution for manufacturing, inventory and marketing.
Products/Services: Forecast Pro.

Business Resource Software, Inc.
2013 Wells Branch Parkway, Suite 305
Austin, Texas 78728
Phone: (800) 423-1228 (512) 251-7541
Email: info@brs-inc.com
WWW: www.brs-inc.com
Contact: Mr. James Brawner
Description: Provides 'Expert System' software for strategy, planning and marketing. Tools embody the knowledge of industry experts like Michael Porter & Philip Kotler in order to provide a detailed analysis. Free evaluation disk.
Products/Services: Business Insight®, Quick Insight™, Plan Write®.

SOFTWARE • INTELLIGENCE/EXPERT/MODELING

Interfacing Technologies Corp.
7575 Trans Canada Highway
Suite 610 Saint-Laurent
Montreal, Quebec H4T 1V6
Canada
Phone: (514) 856-9097
Fax: (514) 856-3377
Email: firststep@interfacing.com
WWW: www.interfacing.com/
Contact: Mr. Artun Kucuk
Description: FirstSTEP is a business process modeling tool that creates a realistic representation of enterprises and dynamically simulates processes, activities, associated resources and workflow, to evaluate performance metrics, bottlenecks, etc.
Products/Services: FirstSTEP.

Mercator Corporation
21 Pleasant Street, Suite 201
Newburyport, Massachusetts 01950
Phone: (800) 997-7627 (978) 463-4093
Fax: (978) 463-9375
Email: info@mercatorcorp.com
WWW: www.mercatorcorp.com
Contact: Ms. Pamela Marshall
Description: SNAP is one of the world's leading software systems for designing and analyzing questionnaires. Surveys can be pen & paper, CAT1, CAP1, email or Web, 2D & 3D charts or statistics.
Products/Services: SNAP-Questionnaire Design & Analysis, Software & Services.

Micrografx, Inc.
7585 SW Mohawk
Tualatin, Oregon 97062
Phone: (503) 692-8162
Fax: (503) 691-2451
Email: Marks@micrograf.com
WWW: www.micrografx.com
Contact: Mr. Mark Stanford
Description: Optima! is an integrated tool for creating presentation-quality process maps, doing discrete-event simulation, modeling behavior and performing "what if?" analysis. Optima! is being used for BPR, TQM and other process improvement endeavors.
Products/Services: Optima!.

Rothschild Strategies Unlimited, LLC
P.O. Box 7568
Wilton, CT 06897-7568
Phone: (203)847-5638
Fax: (203)847-1426
E-mail: sales@strategyleader.com
Web: www.strategyleader.com
Contact: Mr. Bill Rothschild
Description: Focus on attractive segments where competitive advantage can be sustained.
Product/service: StrategyLeader®

Sawtooth Technologies
1007 Church Street
Evanston, Illinois 60201
Phone: (847) 866-0870
Fax: (847) 866-0876
Email: info@sawtooth.com
WWW: www.sawtooth.com
Contact: Mr. Brett Jarvis
Description: PC software for research data collection and analysis: Sensus suite of products for windows-based and multimedia interviewing and conjoint analysis; CATI System for Computer-Aided Telephone Interviewing; seminars and on-site training in conjoint analysis and other research methods; newsletter on computer interviewing and advanced research techniques. Call for brochures and demo disk.
Products/Services: Sensus suite of products.

SPSS, Inc.
444 North Michigan Avenue
Chicago, Illinois 60611-3962
Phone: (312) 329-2400 (312) 467-5245
Email: skalell@spss.com
WWW: www.spss.com
Contact: Ms. Susan Kalell
Description: SPSS for Windows is a powerful easy-to-use, easy to learn statistical package for business or research, featuring top quality statistics, high resolution graphics and revolutionary reporting and distributing capabilities.
Products/Services: SPSS for Windows.

Superior Software, Inc.
16055 Ventura Boulevard, Suite 650
Encino, California 91436-2609
Phone: (800) 421-3264
Fax: (818) 783-5846
WWW: www.superior-software.com/
Contact: Mr. Neal Rimer
Description: Menu-driven, 5 year projections, amortizes, calculates taxes, depreciation, etc.
Products/Services: CF: Cash Flow Analysis.

Synquest, Inc.
3500 Parkway Lane, Suite 555
Norcross, Georgia 30092
Phone: (770) 447-8667
Fax: (770) 447-4995
Email: info@synquest.com
WWW: www.synquest.com
Contact: Mr. Art Brown
Description: Optimum, integrated strategic development for worldwide supply chain management.
Products/Services: Strategic Supply Chain Consulting.

Telusys, Inc.
207 South Racine Avenue
Chicago, Illinois 60607-2882
Phone: (312) 850-2300
Fax: (312) 850-0198
Email: sales@telusys.net
WWW: www.telusys.net
Contact: Ms. Cherre Neitzka, Vice President
Description: Developers of Internet-based software and site management tools.
Products/Services: Software

Wizsoft, Inc.
6800 Jericho Turnpike, Suite 120 W
Syosset, New York 11791
Phone: (516) 393-5841
Email: info@wizsoft.com
WWW: www.wizsoft.com
Contact: Ms. Irina Sered
Description: * WizRule—A data cleansing & data auditing software tool. * WizWhy—A data-mining software tool to reveal patterns in a database and predicts future cases.
Products/Services: WizRule, WizWhy.

Project Management

Avantos Performance Systems
5900 Hollis Street, Suite A
Emeryville, California 94608
Phone: (510) 654-4600
Fax: (510) 654-1276
Email: kerry.lemos@avantos.com
WWW: www.avantos.com
Contact: Mr. Kerry Lemos
Description: Windows based software for tracking, aligning and delegating goals.
Products/Services: ManagePro 3.1.

CFM, Inc.
3 Jeffrey Circle
Bedford, Massachusetts 01730
Phone: (781) 275-5258
Fax: (781) 275-7008
Email: ccordes@teamflow.com
WWW: www.teamflow.com
Contact: Ms. Catherine Cordes
Description: Team project management/deployment flowcharting software.
Products/Services: TeamFlow

Decision Graphics UK, Ltd.
Westfield House, Bonnets Lane
Ifield
Crawley, West Sussex RH11 ONY
United Kingdom
Phone: 44 1293 560056
Fax: 44 1293 610500
Email: marketing@autofm.co.uk
WWW: www.autofm.co.uk
Contact: Ms. Nicola Parker, Marketing Manager
Description: AutoFM Desktop is a complete range of products for the management of people and space. It will help the smallest company to the largest corporations, rapidly solve their changing business needs. Designed for Windows NT/95.
Products/Services: AutoFM Desktop.

Experience in Software, Inc.
2000 Hearst Avenue, Suite 202
Berkeley, California 94709-9944
Phone: (800) 678-7008 (510) 644-0694
Fax: (510) 644-3823
Email: info@projectkickstart.com
WWW: www.projectkickstart.com
Contact: Ms. Carolyn Burd
Description: Instant project planner with Gantt chart/assignments. Microsoft Project compatible.
Products/Services: Project KickStart.

Mesa Systems Guild
60 Quaker Lane
Warwick, Rhode Island 02886
Phone: (401) 828-8500
Fax: (401) 828-9550
Email: info@mesasys.com
WWW: www.mesasys.com
Contact: Ms. Maribeth McNair
Description: Mesa/Vista is a product developer's project and process management forum for sharing information.
Products/Services: Mesa/Vista

Skymark Corporation

7300 Penn Avenue
Pittsburgh, Pennsylvania 15208
Phone: (800) 826-7284 (412) 371-0680
Fax: (412) 371-0681
WWW: www.pathmaker.com
Contact: Mr. Steve David
Description: PathMaker® is the only software on the market which combines project planning and meeting support with the essential tools for process improvement. Tools include flowchart, brainstorm, affinity, cause and effect diagram, mulitvote, weighted criteria rating, structured discussion, force field analysis, control charts, histograms, Pareto analysis and more. Consultants use PathMaker to help clients with Benchmarking, Strategic Planning, and Quality Management. Many consultants also act as PathMaker resellers, with extra revenues from training, facilitation, customization and special projects.
Products/Services: PathMaker.

Software Resource Consultants, Inc.

P.O. Box 38118
Memphis, Tennessee 38183
Phone: (901) 759-7225
Fax: (901) 759-1721
Email: src1@onlinesrc.com
WWW: www.onlinesrc.com
Contact: Mr. Dinesh Sheth
Description: Provide management consulting, strategic planning, software development and systems integration services. Provide experts in wireless and software industry. Provide consulting services and just in time contract resources as needed.
Products/Services: Consulting, Project management, systems development, software development and staffing.

Time & Billing

Barrister Information Systems Corp.
465 Main Street
Buffalo, New York 14203
Phone: (716) 845-5010
Fax: (716) 845-5033
Email: javsales@barrister.com
WWW: www.barrister.com
Contact: Ms. Barbara V. Hooven, Marketing Administrator
Description: Javelan, 100% Windows-based time/billing, financial management.
Products/Services: Javelan® Practice Management System

BQE Software, Inc.
1852 Lomita Boulevard, Suite 208
Lomita, California 90717
Phone: (888) 245-5669 (310) 530-0214
Fax: (310) 530-0184
Contact: Mr. Will Breiholz
Description: Flexible Time-Billing software perfect for any professional consulting office., Includes Crystal Reports to allow for customization of invoices and reports and is Microsoft Access compatible. Web interface and other Remote utilities available for off-site time and expense entry. It accepts unlimited data entry and one license allows 5 networked users.
Products/Services: BillQuick® Version 2.0

Bytepro Corporation
2192 Martin, Suite 220
Irvine, California 92612-1428
Phone: (800) 713-5322 (888) BYT-EPRO
Fax: (800) 411-4472
Email: wendland@bytepro.com
WWW: bytepro.com
Contact: Mr. Brad Wendland
Description: Top Rated Time & Billing program plus much, much more. Does the work of a Time & Billing Program PLUS a client contact program PLUS a calendar/scheduler program PLUS a full featured accounting program. Seamlessly. Automatically. And at a fraction of the cost.
Products/Services: Time & Profit.

TIME & BILLING • SOFTWARE

Commercial Logic, Inc.
One Lyme Common
P.O. Box 380
Lyme, New Hampshire 03768
Phone: (800) 654-0425 (603) 795-2200
Fax: (603) 795-4908
Email: sales@cli-usa.com
WWW: www.cli-usa.com
Contact: Ms. Anne Stanton
Description: Millennium Practice by CLI: Time and expense management, staff budgeting and scheduling, highly flexible custom or standardized billing and in-depth management analysis reporting. Integration: the lastest OLE technology links Millennium to the best-of-breed accounting, contact management and database engine software: Solomon, Great Plains, Platinum, Goldmine, ACT, Microsoft Sequel, Pervasive.

Practice Management Software for the New Millennium

Contact us today to find out more!

800-654-0425

www.CLI-USA.com

Building on Experience!

Specialists since 1985.

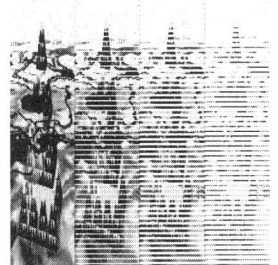

Millennium Practice 2nd Quarter 1999.

Dedicated to meeting the time and project management needs of high end consulting firms.

Commercial Logic, Inc.
ONE LYME COMMON • LYME, NH 03768 • WWW.CLI-USA.COM

Integratech Software
P.O. Box 293403
Lewisville, Texas 75029-3403
Phone: (972) 420-7880
Fax: (972) 420-7880
Email: info@integsoft.com
WWW: www.integsoft.com
Contact: Mr. Randall Fuchs
Description: Time & Billing Software
Products/Services: Bill Central.

Micro Billing Systems, Inc.
117 W Harrison Building #624M
Chicago, Illinois 60605
Phone: (312) 939-1869
Fax: (312) 939-1351
Email: microbilling@worldnet.att.net
WWW: www.microbilling.com/
Contact: Ms. Debra Hines
Description: A complete time and billing system designed to track and allocate staff member time and expenses, to an unlimited number of clients and projects. The option to generate a large number of activity reports including weekly time-sheets, provides a basis for productivity analysis and planning.
Products/Services: Client Project.

Nisus Software
107 South Cedros Avenue
Solana Beach, California 92075
Phone: (800) 890-3030
Fax: (619) 481-7485
Email: sales@nisus.com
WWW: www.nisus.com
Contact: Mr. Joe Murgia
Description: Time & Billing for the Mac & Windows, as well as other products. We also do contract programming.
Products/Services: TimeSlice.

ON-Q Software, Inc.
13764 SW 11 Street
Miami, Florida 33184
Phone: (800) 553-2862
Fax: (305) 220-2666
Email: onqsoftware@compuserve.com
WWW: www.on-qsoftware.com
Contact: Ms. Teri Cajigas
Description: Complete time & fixed fee billing, due date tracking, practice manager and more.
Products/Services: The Accountant's Partner.

Sage U.S., Inc.
17950 Preston Road, Suite 800
Dallas, Texas 75252
Phone: (800) 285-0999 (972) 248-9232
Fax: (972) 248-9245
WWW: www.timeslips.com
Contact: Sales
Description: Time tracking and billing solution for the individual or networked user. Includes customizable billing and reporting features, as well as an optional link to many popular accounting systems.
Products/Services: Timeslips Deluxe.

Sage U.S., Inc.
17950 Preston Road, Suite 800
Dallas, Texas 75252
Phone: (800) 477-6763
Fax: (972) 713-6331
Email: cdsales@sageus.com
WWW: www.timetracking.com
Contact: Sales
Description: Carpe Diem, is the solution for tracking and reporting time, activities and expenses accurately in any large organization.
Products/Services: Carpe Diem.

TRAVEL

Airlines

Aer Lingus Tab
538 Broad Hollow Road
Melville, Rhode Island 11747
Phone: (888) IRISH-AIR (212) 557-1090

Air North America
Phone: (838) 792-4982

Air Ontario
Phone: (800) 776-3000

Airways International
Phone: (305) 876-0170

All Nippon Airways
11 West 50th Street, First Floor
New York, New York 10111
Phone: (800) 235-9262 (202) 857-0909

American Airlines
Consumer Relations
P.O. Box 619612 MD2400
DFW Airport, Texas 75261-9612
Phone: (800) 433-7300 (817) 967-2000
WWW: www.americanair.com
Description: American AAdvantage: 800-882-8880

American Eagle
P.O. Box 619616, MD5494
DFW Airport, Texas 75261-9616
Phone: (800) 433-7300 (817) 963-1234
Fax: (817) 931-5683
WWW: www.aa.com

American Transair
Phone: (800) 825-8538

Arizona Airways
Phone: (800) 274-0662

Arizona Pacific
Phone: (800) 221-7904

Austral Airlines
Phone: (305) 823-4368

Australian
Phone: (800) 922-5122

Avensa-Venezuelan
Phone: (800) 283-6727

Bush Air
Phone: (907) 543-2424

Canadien Airlines International Limited
700 2nd Street SW
Suite 2800
Calgary, Alberta T2P 2W2
Canada
Phone: (905) 612-2657

Carnival Airlines
Phone: (800) 824-7386

TRAVEL • AIRLINES

Chicago Express
Phone: (800) 264-3929

Delta Air Lines
Phone: (800) 221-1212
Description: Delta Skymiles: 800-323-2323

Delta Air Lines
Phone: (800) 241-4141

Delta Airlines
1030 Delta Boulevard, Department 746
P.O. Box 20706
Hartsfield Atlanta International Airport
Atlanta, Georgia 30320-6001
Phone: (800) 241-6108 (404) 715-2600
WWW: www.delta_air.com

Dominicana
Phone: (800) 635-3560

Eastern Express
Phone: (207) 941-6565

El Al Israel Airlines
Phone: (800) 223-6700

Finn Air
Phone: (800) 950-5000

Japan Airlines Company Limited
655 Fifth Avenue
New York, New York 10022-5303
Phone: (212) 310-1344

Key Airlines
Phone: (800) 786-2386

L Express
Phone: (800) 344-1970

Lan Chili
Phone: (800) 735-5526

Lufthansa German Airlines
1640 Hempstead Turnpike
East Meadow, New York 11554-1040
Phone: (800) 645-3880
Description: Miles & More: 800-581-6400

Malaysia Airlines
Phone: (800) 552-9264

Malaysia Airlines
5933 West Century Boulevard #506
Los Angeles, California 90045-5429
Phone: (310) 642-0849

MGM Grand Air
Phone: (800) 933-2646

National Airlines
Phone: (800) 949-9400

Nigeria
Phone: (212) 935-2700

Northwest Airlines
Phone: (800) 225-2525
Description: Worldperks: 800-447-3757

Northwest Worldwide
People's Republic of China
Phone: (800) 225-2525
Description: Worldperks: 800-447-3757

AIRLINES • TRAVEL

Qantas Airways
304 East 45th Street, 6th Floor
New York, New York 10017
Phone: (212) 370-1313
Fax: (212) 370-1159
Contact: Mr. David Heller

Saeta Airlines
Phone: (800) 827-2382

Trump Shuttle
Phone: (800) 247-8486

TWA
Phone: (800) 892-4141

United Airlines
Phone: (800) 538-2929

United Airlines
Phone: (800) 241-6522

USAir
Phone: (800) 622-1015

USAir
Phone: (800) 428-4322

Western Pacific
Phone: (800) 930-3030

Car Rental Agencies

Alamo Rent-A-Car
110 South East 6th Street
P.O. Box 22776
Ft. Lauderdale, Florida 33335
Phone: (800) 327-9633 (954) 522-0000

Allstate Car Rental
5175 Rent-A-Car Road
Las Vegas, Nevada 89119-1229
Phone: (800) 634-6186 (702) 736-6147

Avis International
900 Old Country Road
Garden City, New York 11530-9795
Phone: (800) 331-1084 (516) 222-3000
Products/Services: Wizard.

Budget Rent-A-Car
4225 Naperville Road
Lisle, Illinois 60532
Phone: (800) 527-0700 (708) 955-1900

Dollar Rent-A-Car
5330 East 31st Street
Tulsa, Oklahoma 74153
Phone: (800) 800-4000

Hertz Rent-A-Car
225 Brae Boulevard
Parkridge, New Jersey 07656
Phone: (800) 654-3131 (201) 307-2000
Products/Services: #1 Gold.

National Car Rental System, Inc.
7700 France Avenue South
Minneapolis, Minnesota 55435
Phone: (800) 227-7368 (800) 627-7777
WWW: www.nationalcar.com
Products/Services: Emerald Isle.

Thrifty Car Rental
5330 East 31st Street, Suite 100
P.O. Box 35250
Tulsa, Oklahoma 74153-0250
Phone: (800) 331-3550

Value Rent-A-Car
P.O. Box 5040
Boca Raton, Florida 33431
Phone: (800) 327-2501

Custom Transportation/Charter Aircraft

Charter Fleet International
Presidential Hangar/Sanford Reg. Apt.
Sanford, Maine 04073-6900
Phone: (800) 355-5387
Fax: (207) 490-6900
Email: airchrtr@concentric.net
WWW: www.aircraftcharters.com
Contact: Mr. Philip J. Kemp, Vice President Marketing
Description: Worldwide aircraft management and charter.
Products/Services: Custom transportation/Charter aircraft.

Charter Services-Worldwide
3700 Rio Grande Boulevard NW
Albuquerque, New Mexico 87107
Phone: (505) 761-9000
Fax: (505) 343-7377
Email: charterservices@mindspring.com
WWW: www.chartersvcs.com/
Contact: Ms. Deborah S. Weh
Products/Services: Charter Services - Worldwide.

Executive Jets
85 Chestnut Ridge Road
Montvale, New Jersey 07645
Phone: (800) 821-2299
Products/Services: NetJets.

Art J.O. Horn & Associates
Maria Theresia Strasse 1
Munich, D-81675
Federal Republic of Germany
Phone: 49 89 470 5566
Fax: 49 89 470 6600
Contact: Mr. Art Horn
Description: Personalized chauffeured car tours for private parties from one to seven or more persons with experienced, knowledgeable English-speaking driver/guide. Ancestor tracing and WW II battlefield tours tailored to your requirements. 30 years in business. Highest standard. American references. ASTA Member, American Society of Travel Agents. API member, The Nation's Premier Travel Professionals. Travel Agency co-operation welcome.
Products/Services: Chauffeured Car/Van services

Presidential Limousines
2451 State Street
San Diego, California 92075
Phone: (800) 708-7009
Fax: (619) 702-6142
Email: info@preslimo.com
WWW: www.preslimo.com
Contact: Ms. Rebecca Grenz
Description: Professional ground transportation, specializing in corporate transportation worldwide.
Products/Services: Limousine Service.

Tech Aviation
Wilkes-Barre/Scranton International Airport
Avoca, Pennsylvania 18641
Phone: (717) 457-3000
WWW: www.flightdata.com/techaviation
Contact: Mr. Jim Gallagher
Description: Provide corporate and large commercial jet and turboprop service and contracts throughout North America and Europe.
Products/Services: Tech Aviation Service, Inc.

Frequent Flyer Programs

A O M French Airlines
Phone: (800) 892-9136

Above It All
Phone: (800) 538-7590

Aces
Phone: (800) 846-2237

Action Air Lines
Phone: (800) 243-8623

Adventure Airlines
Phone: (800) 543-3077

Aer Lingus
Phone: (800) 223-6537

Aero California
Phone: (800) 237-6225

Aero Costa Rica
Phone: (800) 237-6274

Aerochago
Phone: (800) 527-9288

Aeroejecutivo Sa-De-Cv
Phone: (800) 735-5396

Aeroflot
Phone: (800) 995-5555

Aeroflot Cargo Sales
Phone: (800) 506-5544

Aerolineas Argentinas
Phone: (800) 333-0276

Aeromar
Phone: (800) 950-0747

Aeromexico
Phone: (800) 237-6639

Aeromexico Club Premier/ Aeromiles
13405 NW Freeway, Suite 111
Houston, Texas 77040
Phone: (800) 247-3737

Aeroperu
Phone: (800) 777-7717

Air Afrique
Phone: (800) 456-9192

Air Alma
Phone: (800) 463-9660

Air Antillean
Phone: (800) 327-7230

Air Aruba
Phone: (800) 882-7822

TRAVEL • FREQUENT FLYER PROGRAMS

Air Aurora
Phone: (800) 443-0478

Air Caledonia
Phone: (800) 677-4277

Air Canada
P.O. Box 15000
Station Airport, Quebec
Canada
Phone: (800) 776-3000
Description: Air Canada Aeroplan: 800-361-5373
Air Canada Aeroplan (US): 800 361-8253

Air Canada Aeroplan
Canada
Phone: (514) 395-0300

Air China
Phone: (800) 986-1985

Air Cruise America
Phone: (800) 359-3237

Air Europa
Phone: (888) 772-4699

Air Fiji
Phone: (800) 677-4277

Air France
142 West 55th Street
New York, New York 10019
Phone: (800) 237-2747 (212) 830-4000
Description: Frequence Plus: 800-237-2747

Air Guadeloupe
Phone: (800) 522-3394

Air India
Phone: (800) 223-2250

Air Inter-French Airlines
Phone: (800) 237-2747

Air Jamaica
Phone: (800) 523-5585

Air Lanka
Phone: (800) 421-9898

Air Madagascar
Phone: (800) 821-3388

Air Margarita
Phone: (800) 326-0339

Air Marshall Islands
Phone: (800) 543-3898

Air Mauritius
Phone: (800) 537-1182

Air Metro
Phone: (800) 871-1000

Air Midwest
Phone: (800) 428-4322

Air Montreal
Phone: (800) 561-4270

Air Namibia
Phone: (800) 361-6210

FREQUENT FLYER PROGRAMS • TRAVEL

Air Nauru
Phone: (800) 998-6287

Air Nevada
Phone: (800) 634-6377

Air New Zealand
1960 East Grand Avenue #900
El Segundo, California 90245-5055
Phone: (800) 262-1234 (310) 648-7000
Description: 64 9 373 4747

Air Pacific
Phone: (800) 227-4446

Air Panama
Phone: (800) 272-6262

Air Paraquay
Phone: (800) 677-7771

Air Sedona
Phone: (800) 535-4448

Air Seychelles
Phone: (800) 677-4277

Air Sunshine
Phone: (800) 327-8900

Air Trails
Phone: (800) 245-9100

Air UK
Phone: (800) 249-2478

Air Ukraine
Phone: (800) 857-2463

Air Vantage
Phone: (800) 279-9383

Air Vanuatu
Phone: (800) 677-4277

Air Vegas
Phone: (800) 255-7474

Air Virginia
Phone: (800) 446-7834

Air Wisconsin
Phone: (800) 241-6522

Air Zaire
Phone: (800) 442-5114

Air Zimbabwe
Phone: (800) 228-9485

Airatlantic Airlines
Phone: (800) 223-5552

Airianka
Phone: (800) 421-9898

Airtran Airways
Phone: (800) AIR-TRAN

Alaska Airlines
Phone: (800) 426-0333
Description: Alaska Mileage Plan: 800-654-5669

Alitalia Premium Program
Phone: (800) 223-5730
Description: Mileage Club: 800-262-4653
All Nippon Airways: 800-235-9262 (reservations)

All Nippon Airways Goldpass
2050 West 190th Street, Suite 100
Torrance, California 90504-6228
Phone: (800) 262-4653

Aloha Airlines, Incorporated
P.O. Box 30028
Honolulu, Hawaii 96820
Phone: (800) 367-5250 (609) 661-0937
Description: AlohaPass: 808-486-7277

Ambassadair
Phone: (800) 225-9919

America West Airlines
Phone: (800) 235-9292
Description: America West FlightFund: 800-247-5691

American Express Membership Rewards/USA
Phone: (800) 297-3276

American International Airways, Inc.
Phone: (800) 521-1590

American Trans Air
Phone: (800) 225-2995

Amerijet International, Inc.
Phone: (305) 593-5500

Ansett Australia Airlines
Phone: (800) 366-1300
Description: Global Rewards: 61-39-6239111

Asiana Airlines
ABC Service Center
3530 Wilshire Boulevard, Suite 145
Los Angeles, California 90010
Phone: (800) 227-4262
Description: Bonus Club: 888-222-4359

Aspen Mountain Air
Phone: (800) 877-3932

Atkin Air
Phone: (800) 924-2471

Atlas Air
Phone: (800) 462-2012

Austrian Airlines
Phone: (800) 843-0002

Avensa/Servivensa Airlines
Phone: (800) 428-3672

Avianca
Phone: (800) 284-2622

Aviateca Guatemala
Phone: (800) 535-4148

Avioimpex-Interimpex
Phone: (800) 713-2622

B A S Airlines
Phone: (800) 245-3248

FREQUENT FLYER PROGRAMS • TRAVEL

Bahamas Air
Phone: (800) 222-4262

Balair/CTA
Phone: (800) 322-5247

Balkan Bulgarian Airlines
Phone: (800) 852-0944

Baltic Int'l Airlines
Phone: (800) 548-8181

Bemidji Airlines
Phone: (800) 332-7133

Best Western Gold Crown Club International
Phone: (800) 237-8483

Big Sky Airlines
Phone: (800) 237-7788

Blue Pacific Air
Phone: (800) 600-0082

Branson Airlines
Phone: (800) 442-4247

British Airways
75-20 Astoria Boulevard
Jackson Heights, New York 11370
Phone: (800) 247-9297 (718) 397-4000
Description: British Airways Executive Club-USA: 800-955-2748

British Airways Executive Club Canada
75-20 Astoria Boulevard
Jackson Heights, New York 1137
Phone: (800) 955-2748
Description: British Airways Executive Club, Canada: 800-463-3932

British Midland Airways
Phone: (800) 788-0555
Description: Diamond Club: 44 133 285 4274 (must be European)

Buffalo Airways
Phone: (800) 268-2944

Business Express Airlines
Phone: (800) 345-3400

BWIA International
Phone: (800) 327-7401

Canada 3000
Phone: (888) 226-3000

Canadian Air International
Phone: (800) 426-7000
Description: Canadian Plus: 800-426-7007

Canadian Plus
Executive Office/Scotia
2800-700 2nd Street, SW
Calgary, Alberta T2P 2W2
Canada
Phone: (800) 426-7007

Cape Air
Phone: (800) 352-0714

2000 Consultants ResourceBook / 179

Casino Airlines
Phone: (888) 227-1177

Cathay Pacific Airways
Phone: (800) 233-2742

Cayman Airways
Phone: (800) 441-3003

Century Airlines
Phone: (800) 541-0410

Chart Air San Juan
Phone: (800) 237-1101

Chautauqua Airlines
Phone: (800) 428-4322

China Airlines
Phone: (800) 227-5118

China Dynasty Flyer
China Airlines Dynasty Flyer Club
6053 West Century Boulevard
Los Angeles, California 90994
Phone: (800) 227-5118

China Eastern Airlines
Phone: (800) 200-5118

Citybird
Phone: (800) 248-9247

Colgan Air
Phone: (800) 272-5488

Comair
Phone: (800) 354-9822

Condor
Phone: (800) 524-6975

Conquest Air
Phone: (800) 722-0860

Continental Airlines
2929 Allen Parkway
Houston, Texas 77210-4607
Phone: (800) 525-0280 (713) 834-5000
Description: Continental OnePass: 713-952-1630
Partner Rewards: 800-344-3333

Copa Airlines
Phone: (800) 892-2672

Corporate Airlines
Phone: (800) 555-6565

Corporate Express-Canada
Phone: (800) 661-8151

Corsair
Phone: (800) 677-4277

Croatia Airlines
Phone: (800) 247-5353

Cyprus Airlines
Phone: (800) 333-2977

Czech Airlines
Phone: (800) 223-2365

FREQUENT FLYER PROGRAMS • TRAVEL

Diners Club Club Rewards
Phone: (800) 234-6377

Direct Air
Phone: (800) 428-0706

Dominicana Airlines
Phone: (800) 327-7240

East-West Airlines
Phone: (800) 354-7471

Eastwinds Airlines
Phone: (800) 644-3592

Ecuatoriana
Phone: (800) 328-2367

Egyptair
Phone: (800) 334-6787

El Al Israel Airlines
Phone: (800) 223-6700

El Al Matmid Club
Phone: (800) 223-6700
Description: 800-223-6700

Emery Worldwide
1 Lagoon Drive
Redwood City, California 94065-1564
Phone: (800) 367-3592

Emirates
New York, New York
Phone: (800) 777-3999

Ethiopian Air
Phone: (800) 445-2733 (800) 433-9677 West

Euram
Phone: (800) 555-3872

Eva Airways
Phone: (800) 695-1188

Evergreen International
Phone: (800) 345-5556

Faucett Peru
Phone: (800) 334-3356

Fine Airlines
Phone: (800) 923-9222

Finnair Plus
Phone: (800) 950-5000
Description: Finnair Plus: 800-950-3387

Frontier Airlines
Phone: (800) 432-1359

Garuda Indonesia
Phone: (800) 342-7832

Grand Aire Express
Phone: (800) 70-Grand

Gulf Air
3555 Timmons Lane
Suite 1100
Houston, Texas 77027
Phone: (888) FLY-GULF (213) 381-3845

Gulf Air
Phone: (800) 553-2824

Gulfstream International Airlines
Phone: (800) 992-8532

Guyana Airways
Phone: (800) 242-4210

Harbor Airlines
Phone: (800) 359-3220

Hawaiian Airlines
Phone: (800) 367-5320
Description: Hawaiian Gold+Plus: 808-838-5333

Hilton Hhonors Worldwide
California
Phone: (972) 788-0878

Holiday Inn Priority Club Worldwide
Phone: (408) 321-2939

Holiday Inn Priority Club Worldwide
Phone: (800) 272-9273

Holiday Inn Priority Club Worldwide
Phone: (800) 272-9273

Holiday Inn Priority Club Worldwide
Phone: (800) 272-9273

Horizon Air
Phone: (800) 547-9308

Hyatt Gold Passport
Phone: (800) 544-9288

Iberia
Phone: (800) 772-4642

Iberia Plus
Phone: (800) 772-4642

Icelandair
Phone: (800) 223-5500

Island Air
Phone: (800) 323-3345

Island Airlines
Phone: (800) 248-7779
Japan
Phone: 81 3 5259 3939

JAL Mileage Bank Americas
655 5th Avenue
New York, New York 10022
Phone: (800) 525-6453

Japan Air Lines
Phone: (800) 525-3663

Jet Express Exec. Charter
Phone: (800) 806-8833

Jet South
Phone: (800) 538-7688

Kenya Airways
Phone: (800) 343-2506

Kiwi Internationanal
Phone: (800) 538-5494

FREQUENT FLYER PROGRAMS • TRAVEL

KLM
Phone: (800) 374-7747
Description: Flying Dutchman: 800-374-7747

KLM Flying Dutchman
Phone: (800) 438-5000
Live in Europe: 31 20 648 7111

Korean Air
Skypass Mileage Program
1813 Wilshire Boulevard, 4th Floor
Los Angeles, California 90057
Phone: (800) 438-5000
Description: Skypass: 800-525-4480

Kuwait Airways
Phone: (800) 458-9248

Lacsa Costa Rica Airlines
Phone: (800) 225-2272

Ladeco Airlines
Phone: (800) 825-2332

Lan-Chile Airlines
Phone: (800) 735-5526

Latinpass
Description: 800-44-LATIN

Lauda Airlines
Phone: (800) 645-3880

Leading Air Logistics
Phone: (800) 552-5323

Liat
Phone: (800) 468-0482

Lloyd Aereo Boliviano
Phone: (800) 327-3098

Lone Star Airlines
Phone: (800) 877-3932

LTU International
Phone: (800) 888-0200

Lufthansa Airlines
P.O. Box 945
Santa Clarita, California 91380
Phone: (800) 645-3880
Description: Miles & More: 800-581-6400

Lynx Air International
Phone: (888) LYNX-AIR

Malev Hungarian
Phone: (800) 223-6884

Mark Air
Phone: (800) 627-5247

Marriott Miles
Phone: (801) 468-4000

Marriott Rewards
United Kingdom
Phone: 44 171 584 5500

Marriott Rewards
Phone: (800) 249-0800

Martinair Holland
Phone: (800) 627-8462

TRAVEL • FREQUENT FLYER PROGRAMS

Mesa Airlines
Phone: (800) 637-2247

Mesaba Airlines
Phone: (800) 225-2525

Mexicana Airlines
9841 Airport Boulevard
Suite #200
Los Angeles, California 90045
Phone: (800) 531-7921
Description: Mexicana Frequenta: 800-531-7901

Middle East Airlines
Phone: (800) 664-7310

Midway Airlines
Phone: (800) 446-4392

Midwest Express Airlines
6744 South Howell Avenue
Oak Creek, Wisconsin 53154
Phone: (800) 452-2022
Description: Frequent Flyer: 800-452-2022

Miles Above
Phone: (800) 469-6453

Mohawk Airlines
Phone: (800) 252-2144

Nantucket Airlines
Phone: (800) 635-8787

Nations Air
Phone: (800) 883-5987

New England Airlines
Phone: (800) 243-2460

Nica Airlines
Phone: (800) 831-6422

Northwest Airlines, Inc.
Department A 1020
5101 Northwest Drive
St. Paul, Minnesota 55111-3034
Phone: (800) 225-2525 (612) 726-2046
Description: Worldperks: 800-447-3757

Northwest Worldperks
Corporate Headquarters, A6910
5101 Northwest Drive
St. Paul, Minnesota 55111-3034
Phone: (800) 225-2525 (800) 327-2881
WWW: www.nwa.com
Description: Worldperks: 800-447-3757

Olympic Airways
Phone: (800) 223-1226

Pacific Coastal Airlines
Phone: (800) 663-2872

Pakistan International Airlines
Phone: (800) 221-2552

Pan AM
Phone: (800) 359-7262
Pan Am WorldPass: 800-662-2068

Pan-AM Air Bridge
Phone: (800) 424-2557

Passages
Phone: (800) 738-4828

Penair
Phone: (800) 448-4226

Philippine Airlines
Phone: (800) 435-9725

Polish Air-Lot
Phone: (800) 223-0593

Polynesian Airlines
Phone: (800) 677-4277

Proair
Phone: (800) 939-9551

Qantas Airways
Phone: (800) 227-4500

Qantas Frequent Flyer
841 Apollo Street
Suite 400
El Segundo, California 90245-4741
Phone: (800) 227-4220

Ramada Business Card
Phone: (800) 672-6232

Reeve Aleutian Airways
Phone: (800) 544-2248

Reno Air
Phone: (800) 736-6247

Rover Airways International
Phone: (800) 828-4668

Royal Air Maroc
Phone: (800) 344-6726

Royal Jordanian Airlines
Phone: (800) 223-0470

Royal Nepal
Phone: (800) 266-3725

Royal Tonga Airlines
Phone: (800) 486-6426

Ryan International Airways
Phone: (800) 727-0457

Sabena
Phone: (800) 955-2000

Saro Airlines
Phone: (800) 538-7276

SAS Eurobonus
Frosundavites Alle 1
Customer Service
Solna, S-19587
Sweden
Phone: 800 437 5807

SAS Scandinavian Airlines
Phone: (800) 221-2350
Description: Eurobonus: 800-221-2350

Saudia Arabian Airlines
Phone: (800) 472-8342

Scenic Airways
Phone: (800) 634-6801

Sheraton Club International
Phone: (800) 247-2582 (513) 248-2672

Silk Air
Phone: (800) 745-5247

Singapore Airlines
Phone: (800) 742-3333

Sky Bus
Phone: (800) 755-9287

Skywest Airlines
Phone: (800) 453-9417

Solomon Airlines
Phone: (800) 677-4277

South African
Phone: (800) 722-9675
Description: Voyager: Press 4, 1-800-722-9675

Southern Air Transport
Phone: (800) 898-4110

Southwest Airlines
P.O. Box 36611
Dallas, Texas 27235-1611
Phone: (800) 435-9792 (214) 792-4000
Description: Rapid Rewards: 800-445-5764

Southwest Company Club
Southwest Airlines, The Company Club
PO Box 36657
Dallas, Texas 75235-1657
Phone: (800) 445-5764

Spanair
Phone: (888) 545-5757

Spirit Airline
Phone: (800) 772-7117

Sun Country Airlines
Phone: (800) 359-5786
Description: Air Rewards: 800-359-5786

Sunflower Airlines, Fiji
Phone: (800) 707-3454

Sunjet
Phone: (800) 4-SUNJET

Suriname Airways
Phone: (800) 327-6864

Swissair
Phone: (800) 221-4750

Swissair/Austrian Qualiflyer
Qualiflyer Service Center C.S. 8910
41 Pinelawn Road
Melville, New York 11747-8910
Phone: (800) 221-8125

Taca Airlines
Phone: (800) 535-8780

Tam-Transportes Aereos
Phone: (888) 235-9826

Tan Sasha Honduras
Phone: (800) 327-1225

FREQUENT FLYER PROGRAMS • TRAVEL

Tap Air Portugal
Phone: (800) 221-7370

Thai Airways
Phone: (800) 426-5204
Description: Frequent Flyer: 800-426-5204 Press 2

Tower Air
Phone: (800) 221-2500

Trans-Jamaican Airlines
Phone: (800) 263-4354

Transbrasil Airlines
Phone: (800) 872-3153

Travelair
Phone: (800) 948-3770

Tropic Air
Phone: (800) 422-3435

Turkish Airlines
Phone: (800) 874-8875

Turks and Caicos Airway
Phone: (800) 845-2161

TWA Airlines
1415 Olive Street, Suite 100
St. Louis, Missouri 63103
Phone: (800) 221-2000 (314) 589-3600
Description: Frequent Flyer: 800-325-4815

Ukraine International Airlines
Phone: (800) 876-0114

United Airlines
1200 Algonquin Road
P.O. Box 66100
Chicago, Illinois 60666
Phone: (800) 241-6522 (847) 700-4000

United Mileage Plus
Customer Relations
P.O. Box 66100
Chicago, Illinois 60666
Phone: (605) 399-2400

US Airways
Phone: (800) 428-4322
Description: USAir Shuttle: 800-428-4322

USA Jet Airlines
Phone: (800) 872-5387

USAir Frequent Traveler
Crystal Park Four
2345 Crystal Drive
Arlington, Virginia 22227
Phone: (800) 872-4738

USAir Inc.
Crystal Park Four
2345 Crystal Drive
Arlington, Virginia 22227
Phone: (800) 428-4322 (202) 223-3430

Vanguard Airlines
Phone: (800) 826-4827

Varig Brazilian Airlines
Phone: (800) 468-2744

Vasp Brazilian Airlines
Phone: (800) 433-0444

Viasa International Airways
Phone: (800) 327-4470

Vietnam Airlines
Phone: (800) 565-2742

Virgin Atlantic
Phone: (800) 862-8621
Description: Frequent Flyer: 800-365-9500

Virgin Freeway
U.S. Virgin Freeway
747 Belden Avenue
Norwalk, Connecticut 06850
Phone: (800) 365-9500

Virgin Freeway
Phone: (800) 862-8621
Description: Frequent Flyer: 800-365-9500

Vision Air
Phone: (888) 4VISAIR

Westin Premier
Phone: (800) 521-2000
Phone: (412) 333-1500

Westjet Airlines
Phone: (800) 538-5696

Wings West Airlines
Phone: (800) 252-0017

World Airways
Phone: (800) 967-5350

Yemen Airways
Phone: (800) 936-3642

Yta Freniva
Phone: (800) 382-4484

Yugoslav Airlines
Phone: (800) 752-6528

Zambia Airways
Phone: (800) 223-1136

Hotels

Marriott
1 Marriott Drive
Washington, District of Columbia 20058
Phone: (800) 228-9290 (301) 380-9000

Renaissance
29800 Bainbridge Road
Cleveland, Ohio 44139
Phone: (800) 468-3571 (216) 498-9090

Westin
Westin Building
2001 6th Avenue
Seattle, Washington 98121
Phone: (800) 228-3000 (206) 443-5000
Contact: Mr. Rick Rosa

Temporary Corporate Housing

The American Property Exchange
2800 Van Ness Avenue
San Francisco, California 94109
Phone: (415) 447-2080
Fax: (415) 441-9296
Email: dbratt@amsisf.com
WWW: www.We-Rent-SanFran.com
Contact: Mr. David Bratt, Marketing Director
Description: A real estate brokerage specializing in rentals and relocation services.
Products/Services: Temporary Corporate Housing

Bridgestreet Accommodations
1896 Georgetown Road
Hudson, Ohio 44236
Phone: (800) B-STREET
Fax: (330) 342-3708
Email: res@bridgest.com
WWW: www.bridgest.com
Contact: Mr. Andy Macy
Description: Throughout the United States, Canada, and London England, BridgeStreet provides beautifully furnished studio, one, two and three bedroom apartments, condominiums and townhouses in downtown or suburban corporate locations to consultants who are on short-term assignment.
Products/Services: Corporate furnished apartments and housing.

Corporate Accommodations of DE, Inc.
1740 Old Coachs Brige Road
Newark, Delaware 19702
Phone: (302) 737-4611
Fax: (302) 737-4612
Contact: Ms. Roslyn Moffitt-Palmer
Description: 1 2 and 3 bedroom apartments, condos, townhouses.
Products/Services: Temporary Corporate Housing.

Elite Corporate Leasing, Inc.
801 SW Third Avenue, Suite 301
Miami, Florida 33130
Phone: (305) 858-9009
Fax: (305) 858-1358
Email: Daryl@fla.net
WWW: www.elite-leasing.com
Contact: Ms. Jenissa Mohammed
Description: Custom furnished apts/houses/condos for a week or longer throughout S. Florida.

Preferred Living
88 Upham Street
Malden, Massachusetts 02148
Phone: (800) 343-2177
Fax: (781) 321-8353
Email: preferredliving@juno.com
WWW: www.preferred-living.com
Contact: Ms. Audrie Bloom, Executive Director
Description: Nation's largest provider of furnished corporate apartments. 30 day minimum.
Products/Services: Temporary Corporate Housing.

Solar World Estates
East 20 Pineridge Court, Suite 7
Spokane, Washington 99208
Phone: (800) 650-6530
Fax: (509) 468-6769
Email: lindal@iea.com
WWW: www.rent.net/ads/solar
Contact: Ms. Linda Longo
Description: We provide everything, fully equipped and furnished (serving Spokane area).

Suite Living
130 N.orth Central Avenue, Suite 320
Phoenix, Arizona 85004
Phone: (800) 554-8464 (602) 256-7360
Email: steliving@aol.com
Contact: Mr. Richard O'Shaughnessy
Description: Providing fully furnished corporate apartments throughout Phoenix and Southern California.
Products/Services: Temporary Corporate Housing.

In consulting, there are leaders and there are followers.
The leaders read CN.

Consultants News has been the industry source since 1970 for:

- News and Analysis
- Best Practices
- Issues and Trends
- Proprietary Data and Research
- Opinion and Insight

Our readers agree...

"...a quick and easy read. We usually pull two or three great ideas out of every issue that are timely to our business."

"...an excellent source of information on management consulting...unequivocally the best source for insight and industry trends and information."

Call today!
800-531-0007 (U.S.)
603-585-6544 (outside U.S.)

For no-risk subscription offer:
subscribe@kennedyinfo.com

CN
CONSULTANTS NEWS
A publication of Kennedy Information

FIRM INDEX

1-800-Batteries, 36

A

A O M French Airlines, 175
A Rao Korukonda, 6
AB Express, 33
ABCTechnologies, Inc., 159
ACSYS Resources, Inc., 38
AH&M Marketing Communications, 25
ASECOSA, 68
Aaron/Smith Associates, Inc., 93
Above It All, 175
Accountmate Software Corporation, 152
Aces, 175
Acquest International L.P., 74
Acsys Resources, Inc., 124
Action Air Lines, 175
Advance Consulting, Inc., 93
Advanced Express, 33
Advanced Information Consultants, Inc., 93
Advanced Technology Advisors, 93
Advantage International, Inc., 10
Adventure Airlines, 175
Adwoa Boateng, 29
Aer Lingus, 175
Aer Lingus Tab, 169
Aero California, 175
Aero Costa Rica, 175
Aerochago, 175
Aeroejecutivo Sa-De-Cv, 175
Aeroflot, 175
Aeroflot Cargo Sales, 175
Aerolineas Argentinas, 175
Aeromar, 175
Aeromexico, 175
Aeromexico Club Premier/ Aeromiles, 175
Aeroperu, 175
Agency Marketing Services, 70
Air Afrique, 175
Air Alma, 175
Air Antillean, 175
Air Aruba, 175
Air Aurora, 176
Air Caledonia, 176

Air Canada, 176
Air Canada Aeroplan, 176
Air China, 176
Air Cruise America, 176
Air Europa, 176
Air Fiji, 176
Air France, 176
Air Guadeloupe, 176
Air India, 176
Air Inter-French Airlines, 176
Air Jamaica, 176
Air Lanka, 176
Air Madagascar, 176
Air Margarita, 176
Air Marshall Islands, 176
Air Mauritius, 176
Air Metro, 176
Air Midwest, 176
Air Montreal, 176
Air Namibia, 176
Air Nauru, 177
Air Nevada, 177
Air New Zealand, 177
Air North America, 169
Air Ontario, 169
Air Pacific, 177
Air Panama, 177
Air Paraquay, 177
Air Sedona, 177
Air Seychelles, 177
Air Sunshine, 177
Air Trails, 177
Air UK, 177
Air Ukraine, 177
Air Vantage, 177
Air Vanuatu, 177
Air Vegas, 177
Air Virginia, 177
Air Wisconsin, 177
Air Zaire, 177
Air Zimbabwe, 177
Airatlantic Airlines, 177
Airborne Express, 33
Airianka, 177
Airtran Airways, 177

FIRM INDEX

Airways International, 169
Alamo Rent-A-Car, 172
Alaska Airlines, 177
Alexander Associates, 124
Alitalia Premium Program, 178
All Nippon Airways, 169
All Nippon Airways Goldpass, 178
Allison, Hull & Malnati, Inc. (AH&M), 19
Allstate Car Rental, 172
Aloha Airlines, Incorporated, 178
Alpha Publications, 82
Ambassadair, 178
America West Airlines, 178
American Airlines, 169
American Consultants League, 53
American Eagle, 169
American Express, 63
American Express Membership Rewards/Canada, 63
American Express Membership Rewards/USA, 178
American International Airways, Inc., 178
American Media, Inc., 56
The American Property Exchange, 190
American Teleconferencing Services, Ltd., 40
American Thermoplastic Company, 19
American Trans Air, 178
American Transair, 169
Amerijet International, Inc., 178
The Amos Tuck School, 119
Anne Klein & Associates, Inc., 26
Ansett Australia Airlines, 178
Applied Marketing Research, Inc., 93
Arizona Airways, 169
Arizona Pacific, 169
Arnold J. Frigeri, 4
Art J.O. Horn & Associates, 173
The Ascher Group, 38
Ashway, Ltd., 124
Asiana Airlines, 178
Aspen Mountain Air, 178
Assessment, Inc., 3, 124
Associates Newsletter Bureau, 25
Association of Management Consulting Firms, 53
Atkin Air, 178
Atlas Air, 178

Audience Insight, LLC, 93
Austral Airlines, 169
Australian, 169
Austrian Airlines, 178
Avantos Performance Systems, 162
Avensa-Venezuelan, 169
Avensa/Servivensa Airlines, 178
Avianca, 178
Aviateca Guatemala, 178
Avioimpex-Interimpex, 178
Avis International, 172
Axon, Inc., 157

B

B A S Airlines, 178
BG & Associates, 126
BQE Software, Inc., 164
BWIA International, 179
Bahamas Air, 179
Baiglobal, Inc., 94
Balair/CTA, 179
Balkan Bulgarian Airlines, 179
Baltic Int'l Airlines, 179
Bar Ilan University, 56
Barnette & Associates/PR Alabama, 25
Barrister Information Systems Corp., 164
Bartels Research Corp., 94
Battelle, 75
Bemidji Airlines, 179
Benedictine University MBA Program, 3
Benefits & Compensation Design Group, 64
Benefit Services, Incorporated, 64
Bentley College, 3
Best Western Gold Crown Club International, 179
Beyen Corporation, 94
Big Sky Airlines, 179
Black Box Catalog, 36
Blaiklock Consulting, 75
Bliss Gouverneur & Associates, 22, 25
Blue Marble Development Group, Inc., 159
Blue Pacific Air, 179
Bob Wright Recruiting, Inc., 145
Bourke & Associates, 94
Bradley Marketing Group, 25
Branson Airlines, 179

Brennan, Thomsen Associates, Inc., 64
Bridgestreet Accommodations, 190
Brindisi Search, 127
British Airways, 179
British Airways Executive Club Canada, 179
British Midland Airways, 179
Bryant College, 3
Budget Rent-A-Car, 172
Buffalo Airways, 179
Bureau Van Dijk Netherlands, 90
Burlington Air Express, 33
The Burnham Research Group, 94
Burton Knowledge Services, 116
Burwell Enterprises, Inc., 82
Bush Air, 169
Business Advantage, Inc., 56
Business Communication Consultants, Inc., 60
Business Development Group, Inc., 40
Business Express Airlines, 179
Business Forecast Systems, Inc., 159
Business Generation Company, 19
Business Resource Software, Inc., 159
Business Trend Analysts, Inc., 94
Byrne Johnson, Inc., 25
Bytepro Corporation, 164

C

CFM, Inc., 162
CHI Research, Inc., 95
CMR Consultancy, Ltd., 95
CRL Network Services Headquarters, 29
CYMRU Insurance Service, 70
Camp, Inc., 68
Canada 3000, 179
Canadian Air International, 179
Canadian Plus, 179
Canadien Airlines International Limited, 169
Cape Air, 179
Carl J. Taylor & Co., 143
Carnival Airlines, 169
Carter McKenzie, Inc., 128
Casino Airlines, 180
Cathay Pacific Airways, 180
Cayman Airways, 180
Century Airlines, 180

Chart Air San Juan, 180
Charter Fleet International, 173
Charter Services-Worldwide, 173
Chautauqua Airlines, 180
Checkmark Software, Inc., 152
Chicago Express, 170
Chicago Graduate School of Business, 120
China Airlines, 180
China Dynasty Flyer, 180
China Eastern Airlines, 180
Citybird, 180
Claritas, Inc., 90
Colgan Air, 180
College Marketing Intelligence, 95
Columbia Business School, 120
Comair, 180
Commercial Logic, Inc., 165
Community-L, Inc., 56
Compensation Resources, Inc., 64
Competitive Intelligence International, 95
Competitive Intelligence Services, Inc., 96
Comprose, 157
Comptrol, Inc., 152
Condor, 180
Confidential Security Services, 96
Conquest Air, 180
Consultant Recruiters, 128
Consultants News, 85
Consultants in Public Relations SA (TAIPEI), 22, 26
Consulting Resource Group, Inc., 128
Contemporary Research, 96
Continental Airlines, 180
Copa Airlines, 180
Copenhagen Business School, 3
Core Software, Inc., 153
Cornell Group International, Consulting, 129
Cornell University, 4
Corporate Accommodations of DE, Inc., 190
Corporate Airlines, 180
The Corporate Directory of U.S. Public Companies, 82
Corporate Express-Canada, 180
Corporate Technology Information Services, 90
Corsair, 180

FIRM INDEX

Cougar Mountain Software, 153
Croatia Airlines, 180
Cyprus Airlines, 180
Czech Airlines, 180

D

D. Frank Research, 99
D. J. Storch & Associates, Inc., 27
DFG Staffing Consultants, Inc., 38
DHL Worldwide Express, 33
Daceasy, Inc., 153
Daniel Wier & Assoc., 144
Darden Graduate School of Business Administration, 120
Data Security Holding, Inc., 96
Data for Decisions in Marketing, Inc., 96
David P. Cordell Associates, 129
De Bellas & Company, 74
De Funiak & Edwards, 129
DeLaura Development Co., L.L.C., 149
Decision Graphics UK, Ltd., 162
Decision Making Research, 96
Delta Air Lines, 170
Delta Airlines, 170
Deyo Group/Online, 29
Diana Jovanovic, 72
Dieckmann & Associates, Ltd., 129
Diners Club Club Rewards, 181
Dinte Resources, Inc., 129
Direct Air, 181
Direct Information Access Corporation, 97
The Directory of Management Consultants, 82
Disaster Recovery Yellow Pages, 83
Diversified Human Resource Services, 65
Dr. James W. Fairfield-Sonn, 4
Dr. Karen Otazo, 59
Dodge Business Research Consulting, 97
Dollar Rent-A-Car, 172
The Domani Group, 97
Dominicana, 170
Dominicana Airlines, 181
Drinkwater Executive Search, 129
Drummond Associates, Inc., 130
Duncan Direct Associates, 19
Dupont Investigative Group, 97

E

E-Strategy, 155
East-West Airlines, 181
Eastern Express, 170
Eastwinds Airlines, 181
Ecuatoriana, 181
Effective Compensation, Inc., 65
Egghead, 36
Egyptair, 181
Eisen & Associates, 26
El Al Israel Airlines, 170, 181
El Al Matmid Club, 181
Elite Corporate Leasing, Inc., 190
Emery Worldwide, 181
Emirates, 181
Entrepreneurial Strategies, 4
Ethiopian Air, 181
Ethos Consulting, Inc., 130
Euram, 181
Eureka—Competitive Intelligence, 97
Euromonitor International, 97
Eva Airways, 181
Evergreen International, 181
Exec Tech, Inc., 130
Executive Jets, 173
Executive Office Assistance, 70
Executive Partners, Inc., 131
Executive Search Plus, Inc., 131
The Executive Source, Inc., 38
Experience in Software, Inc., 162
Explorations, 97

F

FM Staffing, Inc., 38
Facilitate.com, 40
Farin & Assoc., Inc., 154
Faucett Peru, 181
Federal Express, 33
Feedback Marketing Services Pvt., Ltd., 98
Feedback Marketing Services, Inc., 98
Fidelity Graphics, Inc., 36
The Field House, Inc., 98
Find/SVP, Inc., 98
Fine Airlines, 181
Finn Air, 170
Finnair Plus, 181
The Finnie Group, 57

FIRM INDEX

The Finsure House, Inc., 70
First Market Research, 98
First Principals, Inc., 98
Fisher School of Business, 120
Foia Group, Inc., 98
Forbes Custom Publishing, 81
The Ford Group, Inc., 132
Foy, Schneid & Daniel, Inc., 132
Francesca Moscatelli, 107
Frontier Airlines, 181
Fuessler Group, Inc., 26
The Fuqua School of Business, 120

G

G + A West, 20
GOIC, 68
Gale Research, 83
Gardner Carton & Douglas, 76
Garuda Indonesia, 181
General Management Services, Inc., 68
Gerald Linda & Associates, 20
The Georgetown University School of Business, 120
Gilbert Tweed Associates, Inc., 132
Global Computer Supplies, 36
Global Travel Apartments, 155
Goal/QPC, 83
The Goizueta Business School of Emory University, 120
Grace & St. Peter's Chinese Language School, 72
Graduate School of Industrial Administration, 120
Grand Aire Express, 181
Greene International, 99
Greenwood Consulting Services, 65
Greyhound Package Express, 33
Griggs-Anderson Research, 99
Gulf Air, 181, 182
Gulfstream International Airlines, 182
Guyana Airways, 182

H

H. L. Goehring & Associates, Inc., 65
HR & S Consulting, 10
HRD Consultants, Inc., 134
Halbrecht & Company, 132
Hale Assoc., 132
Harbor Airlines, 182
Harper Hewes, Inc., 133
Hart & Associates, Inc., 57
Harvard University, 120
Hawaiian Airlines, 182
The Hawver Group, 76
Heartland Information Services, 11
Hedlund Corp., 133
Heidrick & Struggles, Inc., 134
The Helicon Group, 99
Herbert Kierulff, 5
Hertz Rent-A-Car, 172
Heskes & Partners, 100
Higbee Associates, Inc., 134
Highsmith & Charnock, Inc., 100
Hilton Honors Worldwide, 182
Hisako Sato MacQueen, 72
Hispanic North American Center, 4
Holiday Inn Priority Club Worldwide, 182
Horizon Air, 182
Horton Int'l., 133
Howard Bowen Consulting, 127
Human Resource Development Press, 57
Human Resources Management Hawaii, Inc., 134
Hyatt Gold Passport, 182
The Hyde Group, Inc., 134

I

IBPC, Inc., 5
IMD-International Institute for Management Development, 58
INMAC, 36
Iberia, 182
Iberia Plus, 182
Icelandair, 182
Impact Business Startup, 69
Indiana University At Bloomington, 121
Infoimage, Inc., 158
Information Counselors, Inc., 26
Information Management Consultants, 100
Information Plus, 100
Information Professionals Institute Seminars, 58
Information Resource Services, Inc., 100
Infosearch Zurich GMBH, 100

FIRM INDEX

Infoservice Group, 101
Infosmith Research Services, 101
Infotree, Inc., 101
Innovative Media Research LLC, 101
Insights & Directions, 101
Institute for Intellectual Capital Research, 5
Institute of Management Consultants, 54
Integratech Software, 165
Integrated Software Solutions, 102
Intelliquest Information Group, Inc., 102
The Intellworks—Telemarketer Training & Phone Research, 58
Intercon Research Associates, Ltd., 103
Interdevelopment Oy, 69
Interfacing Technologies Corp., 160
International Council of Management Consulting Institutes, 54
International Events, Inc., 24
International Market Research Information (IMRI), 90
International Survey Research Corporation, 103
Inthesis Development Co., Inc., 103
The Investext Group, 91
Ion, Incorporated, 103
Island Air, 182
Island Airlines, 182

J

J. L. Kellogg School of Management, 121
JAL Mileage Bank Americas, 182
JDG Associates, Ltd., 135
Jack Richman & Associates, 141
James L. Fisk & Associates, 132
Jamieson Consulting Group, 5
Japan Air Lines, 182
Japan Airlines Company Limited, 170
Japan Market Resource Network, 103
Jardine Group Services Corporation, 70
Jay Gaines & Company, Inc., 132
Jeanneret & Associates, Inc., 5
Jere E. Yates & Associates, 8
Jet Express Exec. Charter, 182
Jet South, 182
Joanne E. Ratner Search, 140
John E. Anderson Graduate School of Management, 119
John Jay & Company, 65

John Steiger Financial Services, 67
The Jonathan Stevens Group, Inc., 135
Johnson Graduate School of Management, 121
Jones-Parker/Starr, 135
Jossey-Bass/Pfeiffer, 83
The Journal of Management Consulting, Inc., 86

K

KLM, 183
KLM Flying Dutchman, 183
KPA Associates, Inc., 38
KSA (Kalman, Saffran Associates), Inc., 16
Kalorama Information, 83
Katherine R. Kraemer, 11
Katzman Insurance Agency, 71
Kelley Chunn & Associates, 26
Kenan-Flagler Business School, 121
Kennedy Information Research Group, 89
Kenya Airways, 182
Key Airlines, 170
Kirk Tyson International, Ltd., 115
Kiwi Internationanal, 182
Klemm & Associates, 77
Korean Air, 183
Korey International Ltd., 5
Korn/Ferry International, 135
Krannert GRaduate School of Business, 121
Kurtz Pro-Search, Inc., 136
Kuwait Airways, 183

L

L Express, 170
L. C. Williams & Associates, Inc., 28
L. Gelfin Associates, 99
LBS Associates, 104
LTU International, 183
LaVallee & Associates, 136
Lacsa Costa Rica Airlines, 183
Ladeco Airlines, 183
Lan Chili, 170
Lan-Chile Airlines, 183
Latham International, Ltd., 136
Latinpass, 183
Lauda Airlines, 183
Lawrence Executive Search, 136
Leading Air Logistics, 183

Lee Stephens & Associates, 67
Leon A. Farley Associates, 132
Leonard N. Stern School of Business, 121
The Lett Group, 58
Liat, 183
Library Technology Alliance, Ltd., 91
Lifter & Assoc., 136
Littman & Associates, 27
Lloyd Aereo Boliviano, 183
Loan Pricing Corporation, 104
The Londre Company, Inc., 27
Lone Star Airlines, 183
Lufthansa Airlines, 183
Lufthansa German Airlines, 170
The Lukaszewski Group, Inc., 27
Lynx Air International, 183
Lyons & Associates, 74

M

M. A. Raphael & Associates, 45
M. L. Tawney & Associates, 143
MB, Inc. Executive Search, 137
MGM Grand Air, 170
MIT Sloan School of Management, 6
MJL International, Inc., 69
McCarty Kilian & Company, 6
The McCormick Group, 138
McEachin & Associates, Ltd., 106
McGarry Consulting, 106
Macro International, Inc., 104
Macwarehouse (PC Warehouse), 36
Mail Boxes Etc., 33
Maister Associates, 77
Malaysia Airlines, 170
Malev Hungarian, 183
Management Consultant Network International, 29
Management Recruiters of Bonita Springs, Inc., 137
Management Recruiters, 136
Management Research & Planning Corporation, 104
Management Solutions, Inc., 66
Maritz Marketing Research, Inc., 105
Mark A. Mishken, 6
Mark Air, 183
Market IQ, Inc., 91

Marketing Intelligence Corporation, 105
Marriott, 189
Marriott Miles, 183
Marriott Rewards, 183
Marriott Rewards, 183
The Marsee Group, 60
Martin Stevens Tamaren & Assoc., Inc., 137
Martinair Holland, 183
Matterform Media, 30
Mature Marketing & Research, 106
Maximizer Technologies, Inc., 156
Mercator Corporation, 160
Mesa Airlines, 184
Mesa Systems Guild, 162
Mesaba Airlines, 184
Metromark, 107
Mexicana Airlines, 184
Meyer Associates, Inc., 138
Michael G. Kessler & Associates, Ltd., 104
Michael H. Schuster, 66
Michael P. Sabiers, Ph.D., 6
Michigan School of Business Administration, 122
Micro Billing Systems, Inc., 165
Micrografx, 150
Micrografx, Inc., 160
Microsystems, 9
Midas Management, Inc., 138
Middle East Airlines, 184
Midway Airlines, 184
Midwest Express Airlines, 184
Miles Above, 184
Mohawk Airlines, 184
Moneysoft, Inc., 150
Montenido Associates, 138
Morris Graphics, Inc., 37

N

NCA Associates, 6
Nagler, Robins & Poe, Inc., 138
Nantucket Airlines, 184
National Airlines, 170
National Bureau of Certified Consultants (NBCC), 54
National Car Rental System, Inc., 172
National Consultant Registry, LLC, 20

FIRM INDEX

National Insurance Professionals Corporation, 71
National Management Services, 107
National Search, Inc., 138
National Speakers Association, 54
Nations Air, 184
Navarro, Kim & Associates, 23
Networkmci Conferencing, 40
New England Airlines, 184
New Resi Data Marketing, Inc., 20
Nexus Consultants to Management, 77
Nica Airlines, 184
Nigeria, 170
Nisus Software, 165
Northwest Airlines, 170
Northwest Airlines, Inc., 184
Northwest Worldperks, 184
Northwest Worldwide, 170
Nutmeg Systems Corporation, 16

O

O'Brien & Bell, 139
O'Brien Consulting Services, 140
O'Conor, Wright Wyman, Inc., 74
ON-Q Software, Inc., 166
The Office Alternative, 35
Office Centre, 35
Olney Associates, Inc., 66
Olympic Airways, 184
Onesource Information Services, 91
The Onstott Group, 140
Open Door Software, 151
Open Systems, Inc., 154
Options for Change, 10
Organization Consultants, Inc., 66
Organization Transitions, Inc., 77
Out of Your Mind . . . and Into the Marketplace™, 155

P

P. K. Data, Inc., 107
PC Connection, Inc., 36
PC Zone (Mac Zone), 36
PCM Consulting Group, 86
PEP Enterprises, 49
PEP Enterprises, 55
PKT Consulting Forum, 6

The PRS Group, 69
PSINet, 30
Pacific Coastal Airlines, 184
Pakistan International Airlines, 184
Palisade Corporation, 151
Pan AM, 184
Pan-AM Air Bridge, 184
Paragon Company, 20
Partners in Human Resources International, Inc., 59
The Partnership Group, 140
Passages, 184
Paul Winston Norman & Assoc., 139
Paul-Tittle Associates, Inc., 140
Penair, 185
Penn Consulting Group, 108
Penton Research Services, 108
Perception International, Ltd., 108
Performance Plus, 108
Personnel Decisions, 77
Peters & Associates, Inc., 59
Philip G. Ryan, Inc., 27
Philippine Airlines, 185
Picturetel Corporation, 40
Pinkerton Consulting Services, 109
Planasyst, 59
Polish Air-Lot, 185
The Pollack PR Marketing Group, 27
Polycom, Inc., 41
Polynesian Airlines, 185
Porter & Associates, 109
Power Systems Research, 109
Preferred Living, 190
Presidential Limousines, 173
Prince Market Research, 109
Printovation, 158
Proair, 185
Productivity Press, 59
Professional Support, Inc., 39
Projections, Inc., 109
Protech India, Ltd., 110
Purolator Courier, 33

Q

Qantas Airways, 171, 185
Qantas Frequent Flyer, 185
Quality Controlled Services, 110

FIRM INDEX

R

R. Gaines Baty Associates, Inc., 126
Radford University, 6
Rainmaker Management Consulting, 110
Ralston Purina Company, 110
Ramada Business Card, 185
Randall T. Wert, 73
The Ransford Group, 140
Ray & Berndtson, 140
Razzino-Claymore Associates, 140
Real Trends, Inc., 110
Reeve Aleutian Airways, 185
Renaissance, 189
Reno Air, 185
Research Online International, Inc., 111
Research Solutions, 111
Rev. Fr. Brian S. Bainbridge, 3
Rhodeback & Associates, 66
Richard Kinser & Associates, 135
Richardson Consulting Group, 111
Rincon & Associates, 111
Robert Bennett Associates, 75
Robert L. Sauer Associates, 66
Robert T. Morton Associates, Inc., 39
Rodenberg Tillman & Associates B.V., 111
Roller Marketing Research, 111
Ronald Levitt Associates, 26
The Roper Center for Public Opinion Research, 91
Roper Starch Worldwide, 112
Roth Research, 112
Rothschild Strategies Unlimited, LLC, 160
Rover Airways International, 185
Royal Air Maroc, 185
Royal Jordanian Airlines, 185
Royal Nepal, 185
Royal Tonga Airlines, 185
The Rubicon Group, 141
Russign Servicco, 72
Ryan International Airways, 185

S

SAS Eurobonus, 185
SAS Scandinavian Airlines, 185
SCSD, Inc., 141
SPSS, Inc., 161
Sabena, 185
Saeta Airlines, 171
Sage U.S., Inc., 156, 166
Sakson & Taylor, Inc., 30
Sales Consultants of Princeton, Inc., 141
Sanchez & Levitan, 21
Santangelo Consultants, Inc., 141
Saporito & Associates, Inc., 112
Saro Airlines, 185
Saudia Arabian Airlines, 185
Savoy Partners, Ltd., 141
Sawtooth Technologies, 161
Sbarra & Company, Inc., 66
Scenic Airways, 185
Search America, Inc., 142
Search Corporation, 112
Seco & Zetto Assoc., Inc., 142
Selz/Seabolt Communications, Inc., 27
Senior Level Communications, 21
Service D'Information Industrielle du Quebec, 112
Shafran, Ltd., 112
Sharp Information Research, 116
Sheraton Club International, 186
Sherwood Partners, Inc., 78
Shifra Kilov, 72
Siebrand-Wilton Associates, Inc., 74
Sierra Market Research, 113
Signature Software, Inc., 151
Silk Air, 186
Singapore Airlines, 186
Sky Bus, 186
Skymark Corporation, 163
Skywest Airlines, 186
Sloan School of Management, 122
Smart Solutions Marketing Inc., 22
Software Resource Consultants, Inc., 163
Sokolov Yelena, 72
Solar World Estates, 191
Solomon Airlines, 186
Solution Engineering, 113
South African, 186
Southern Air Transport, 186
Southwest Airlines, 186
Southwest Company Club, 186
Southwestern Professional Services, 39
Spanair, 186
Spear-Izzo Assoc., 142
Spencerstuart, 142

FIRM INDEX

Spirit Airline, 186
Standard & Poor's DRI, 113
Stanford Graduate School of Business, 122
The Stark Wilton Group, 142
Stat One Research, 113
Stax Research, Inc., 113
Steve Lombardo & Associates, 136
Steven D. Norton, 66
Strategic Analysis, Inc., 113
Strategic Executives, Inc., 142
Sue Canney Davison, 4
Suite Living, 191
Sun Country Airlines, 186
Sunflower Airlines, Fiji, 186
Sunjet, 186
Superior Software, Inc., 161
Suriname Airways, 186
The Survey Center, Inc., 114
Suzanne M. Zeng, 73
Swissair, 186
Swissair/Austrian Qualiflyer, 186
Synapse Human Resource Consulting Group, 67
Synergistics Assoc., Ltd., 142
Synquest, Inc., 155, 161
System Technology Group, 154
Systematic Solutions, 154
Systems View, 114

T

TCG Cerfnet, 15
TWA Airlines, 187
TWA, 171
Taca Airlines, 186
Tam-Transportes Aereos, 186
Tan Sasha Honduras, 186
Tap Air Portugal, 187
Team Quality Development, Inc., 59
Tech Aviation, 174
Technology Market Development Company (TMD), 114
Teleconnect, Inc., 92
Teltech Resource Network Corporation, 114
Telusys, Inc., 161
Texas Graduate School of Business, 123
Thai Airways, 187

Thomas Register of American Manufacturers, 84
Thomas Taveggia, 7
Threshold Information, Inc., 114
Thrifty Car Rental, 172
Timothy G. Potter & Associates, 109
Topeka, 30
Tower Air, 187
Trans-Jamaican Airlines, 187
Transbrasil Airlines, 187
Travelair, 187
Triad Consultants, Inc., 67
Tropic Air, 187
Trump Shuttle, 171
Turkish Airlines, 187
Turks and Caicos Airway, 187

U

US Airways, 187
USA Jet Airlines, 187
USAir, 171
USAir Frequent Traveler, 187
USAir, 171
USAir, Inc., 187
Ukraine International Airlines, 187
United Airlines, 171, 187
United Mileage Plus, 187
United Parcel Service, 34
Universes Network, 30
University of Ballarat, 7
University of California At Berkeley (HAAS), 123
University of Chicago, 7
University of Maryland at College Park, 123
University of New Haven, 7
University of Rochester, 123
University of SW Louisiana, 7
University of Southern California, 7
University of Warwick, 7
Urech & Associates, Inc., 115

V

Value Rent-A-Car, 172
Vanguard Airlines, 187
Varig Brazilian Airlines, 187

FIRM INDEX

Vasp Brazilian Airlines, 187
Velocity Business Publishing, Inc., 84
Vermont Specialty Products, Inc., 23
Viasa International Airways, 188
Vietnam Airlines, 188
Virgin Atlantic, 188
Virgin Freeway, 188
Vision Air, 188
Vista Satellite Communications, Inc., 41

W

WMS & Company, Inc., 67
Walden Personnel Testing, 67
Waterford Executive Group, Ltd., 144
Watson International, Inc., 144
Webminer, 115
Weinstein & Company, 144
West/Marketing Associates, 156
Western Pacific, 171
Westin, 189
Westin Premier, 188
Westjet Airlines, 188
The Wharton School, 123
Wilcove Associates, Inc., 92
William D. Criddle, Ph.D., 57
William E. Hay & Company, 133
Wilson-Douglas-Jordan, 145
The Wilson Group, 10
Wings West Airlines, 188
Wizsoft, Inc., 161
Woelfel Research, Inc., 115
Wolfbayne Communications, 22
World Airways, 188

Y

Yale University School of Management, 123
Yemen Airways, 188
The Youth Research Company, 115
Yta Freniva, 188
Yugoslav Airlines, 188

Z

Zambia Airways, 188
Zero Foundation, 10, 115
Zigman-Joseph-Stephenson, 28
Zoom Systems, Inc., 154
Zweig White & Associates, Inc., 86

ADVERTISER INDEX

Association of Management Consulting Firms AMCF 53
Axon, Inc. 157
R. Gaines Baty Associates, Inc. 126
Howard Bowen Consulting 127
BQE Software Inc. 164
Commercial Logic, Inc. 165
Consultant Recruiters 128
Consultants News 85, 192
Consulting Resource Group, Inc. 125
DeLaura Development Co., L.L.C. 149
Duncan Direct Associates 19
Executive Partners Inc. 131
Forbes Custom Publishing .... Inside Back Cover
Gardner, Carton & Douglas 76
Hedlund Corporation 133
Institute of Management Consultants 54
International Events, Inc. 24
The Journal Of Management Consulting, Inc. 86
Kennedy Information Research Group 89
Mature Marketing & Research 106
MB Inc. Executive Search 137
The McCormick Group 139
William M. Mercer .... Back Cover
Micrografx 150
Penn Consulting Group 108
Sharp Information Research 116
Sherwood Partners, Inc. 78
Stax Research, Inc. .... Inside Front Cover
Carl J. Taylor & Co. 143
The Amos Tuck School 119
University of Michigan Business School 122
Waterford Executive Group, Ltd. 144

204 / Copyright © Kennedy Information, LLC • All Rights Reserved